C. S. LEWIS
and the
BRIGHT SHADOW
of
HOLINESS

C. S. LEWIS
and the
BRIGHT SHADOW
of
HOLINESS

GERARD REED

Beacon Hill Press of Kansas City
Kansas City, Missouri

Copyright 1999
by Beacon Hill Press of Kansas City

ISBN 083-411-7525

Printed in the
United States of America

Cover Design: Ted Ferguson

10   9   8   7   6   5   4   3   2   1

To my parents,
Paul and Lucile Reed,
who have for nearly 60 years
encouraged and supported me

and to the memory
of my Aunt Edith Lantz
who gave her life to editing
Nazarene Publishing House
curriculum materials
and who encouraged me
to read and write on the Holy Spirit

Contents

Preface

*F*EW 20TH-CENTURY FIGURES have more pervasively influenced Christendom than C. S. Lewis. His books continue to sell well 35 years after his death. The six volumes of *The Chronicles of Narnia* stud each year's list of best-selling children's stories. *Mere Christianity* continues to sell in Christian bookstores and is on the shelves of most secular outlets as well. No other Christian writer's books have been so continuously in print or so widely sold. And few, if any, writers have so effectively helped evangelize non-Christians (such as Chuck Colson), who acknowledge Lewis's theological insight for helping open them to God's grace.

In a September 1996 issue of *Christianity Today* devoted to "Movers and Shapers of Modern Evangelicalism," John Stackhouse Jr. reviewed the most influential books published since World War II and noted that "one author's books indisputably affected American evangelicals during this period more than . . . any of the other authors mentioned."[1] Ironically, though neither an American nor an "evangelical" as conventionally defined, that author is Lewis! He made a "colossal impact upon a generation and more who sought practical wisdom, digestible theology, wit, verve, logic, and imagination."[2]

A recent column in *Christianity Today* by Charles Colson, "The Oxford Prophet," contends that Lewis is "a true prophet for our postmodern age."[3] The Oxford don's writing not only "pierced the heart of this White House hatchet man," Colson says, but also helped him envision "the ministry of Prison Fellowship," which he now heads. Lewis was such a prophetic thinker, Colson suggests, because he was so deeply immersed in history that he could incisively critique "the narrow confines of the world-view of his own age." Primarily, he thought and wrote from within what he called "the great body of Christian thought down the ages."[4]

A prophet he may well be, but Lewis never claimed status as more than a "lay theologian." Having read many theologians, however, I'm persuaded he understood Christianity better than many who occupy prestigious seminary chairs. What he did claim to do was to clearly explain the traditional Christian faith, and his thoroughly grounded faith informed virtually all he wrote. His was a thoroughly converted mind!

Similarly, though he never devoted a sustained treatise to "holiness," his works include a mass of material concerning it just because holiness of heart and life is one of the central concerns of traditional Christianity. Most clearly, I think, Lewis's emphasis on "transformation," the divine working of the Holy Spirit, infusing grace and conforming believers to the image of Christ Jesus, squares with the call to holiness that is central to the Wesleyan tradition. One finds in him an emphasis upon both the "crisis" moments of decision, grace-sustained choices that chart life's directions, and the supernatural "growth" process that slowly builds character. So while he cannot be packed into a tidy compartment in the "holiness tradition," his thoughts about God, creation, sin, and salvation all support and shed light on holiness themes.

This book, *C. S. Lewis and the Bright Shadow of Holiness,* tries to mix several elements. In part it often resembles an anthology of Lewis quotations, for he is eminently quotable! One of my main struggles was to decide which quotation to leave out, or how much to delete from one included. Amply quoting one whose thought and expression far surpasses my own is, of course, fully justified! Indeed, if I can dangle a literary lure before the reader that will lead him or her to follow up a brief selection and read more of Lewis, one of my goals will be realized.

Second, this book, by virtue of the items selected, tries to interpret Lewis's thought, to place it in categories that (though not necessarily pronounced in his work) seem to help us understand his views on the subject addressed. Here I have tried to be fair, to not impose my presuppositions or expectations on him. I simply hope I have been true to Lewis's basic views. Still, since I looked for his ideas on holiness, it is likely I read into some of his statements more than is actually there! But such is the nature of such endeavors!

Third, his words regularly stimulate me to add insights and comments from noted theologians and thinkers, as well as many of my own, which I trust are true to the basic thrust of his views. Lewis was solidly rooted in mainstream, consensual traditions of the Christian Church, and I seek to show how his views square with the truly formative thinkers of the past, such as Augustine and Thomas Aquinas. Nevertheless, such ideas must be understood to be purely my own ruminations and expositions, which I hope illustrate or expand on Lewis's stance.

I am indebted to Point Loma Nazarene University for a sabbatical leave, which enabled me to write the text, and to the university's "Wesley Center" for a special grant to help subsidize the endeavor.

≥ PART ONE ≤

THE "BRIGHT SHADOW"
OF HOLINESS

1 Heavenly Tracings of a Holy One

"The 'Bright Shadow' of Holiness"

It was as if I were carried sleeping across the frontier, or as if I had died in the old country and could never remember how I came alive in the new. For in one sense the new country was exactly like the old. . . . But in another sense all changed. I did not yet know (and I was long in learning) the name of the new quality. . . . I do now. It was Holiness.[1]

AS A CHILD, C. S. LEWIS NOW AND THEN glimpsed a glowing, truer-than-life world, a realm drenched with the dawn dew of what he could only call "joy." Those moments aroused within him a lingering hunger for richer encounters, a solid toehold, an unending immersion in its glory. In his spiritual autobiography, *Surprised by Joy,* he celebrated the critical threshold he crossed when he purchased a copy of George MacDonald's *Phantases.* While reading it—the story of a young man's spiritual journey that was punctuated by the arresting, life-transforming presence of a "shadow"—Lewis's heart quickened. His earlier encounters with "joy" had seemed like passing excursions through distant realms, disconnected from the world around him. "But now I saw the bright shadow coming out of the book into the real world and resting there, transforming all common things and yet itself unchanged. Or, more accurately, I saw the common things drawn into the bright shadow."[2]

Consequently, he remembered: "That night my imagination

was, in a certain sense, baptized; the rest of me, not unnaturally, took longer. I had not the faintest notion what I had let myself in for by buying *Phantases.*"[3] While reading MacDonald, Lewis sensed a part of his heart worth warming—glowing like a camp-fire in a distant forest—and he found a reality worth living to embrace. Years passed before he became a Christian, but he had basked in a "joy" that surpassed all understanding. From then on he now and again sensed that only its truth, goodness, and beauty would fully satisfy his heart hunger, that mysterious *sehn-sucht* (a German word he sometimes used that is best translated "homesickness" or "longing") for eternal realms that welled up and allured him.

> ## *Lewis sensed a part of his heart worth warming—glowing like a campfire in a distant forest.*

We, too, long for a realm wholly other than our time-bound, earthly existence. Thus we struggle with a modern world that has, in its thoroughly materialistic worldview, sought to ignore the supernatural. The post-Christians Lewis addressed in many of his works had, at the most basic level, rejected the reality of holiness. In its most elemental sense, "holy" means "set apart." That "set apart" heavenly realm has few spokesmen, even in the modern Church! Yet Lewis, in works such as *Miracles,* sought to revive our awareness of supernatural realities, and therein to discover lasting joy.

The core of what Lewis called joy "was Holiness."[4] In his imaginary work, *The Great Divorce,* published a decade before his autobiography, Lewis described meeting MacDonald, who served as his guide heavenward. He remembered that "frosty afternoon at Leatherhead Station when I first bought a copy of *Phantases* (being then about sixteen years old) had been to me what the first sight of Beatrice had been to Dante: 'Here begins the new Life.'"[5] Years passed while he confined such intimations to "the region of the imagination merely," but "slowly and reluctantly" he edged toward Christian faith, ultimately admitting "that the true name of the quality which first met me in his books is Holiness."[6]

The fleeting joys he had earlier felt were rooted in a fundamental joy that is holy. To attain joy through an immersion in the reality of holiness—to find an ultimate good whose taproot bores into the holy, to see truth blazing like a planet in the bright rays of holiness, to delight in beauty as the delicate etchings of the Holy One—inspired much of Lewis's life and thought. To know the Holy One—and through that relationship to be made holy—attracted and transformed him. From all sides, again and again, the melodic notes of a holy singer cried out for his attention.

Now and then we, like the young Lewis, see traces of divinity, shadows of mysterious presences, haunting remnants of things older and deeper and better than ourselves, totally transcending the cramped corridors of our own world. At unexpected moments we feel as if we're stumbling through a darkened "haunted house" or strolling alone on a moonless night through an ancient, fog-swathed cemetery. There is more to the world than meets the eye! Along with Augustine, we wonder: "What is it which gleams through me and smites my heart without wounding it? I am both a-shudder and a-glow. A-shudder, in so far as I am unlike it, a-glow in so far as I am like it."[7]

The word holy means spiritual health.

To Augustine, as to Lewis, what stirs us most deeply is that which is most holy. Strangely enough, though the word *holy* means spiritual health, it produces strongly negative reactions in many. It is as if sick-unto-death people, cancer-ward patients, would forbid doctors and nurses to mention health and well-being! Holiness has unfortunately lost its sheen, its attractiveness. It seems caked with mold and shrouded with funeral flowers, more suitable for eulogies than awards ceremonies, more dreary than delightful. What should be one of the most attractive words in our language has frequently been perverted, turned into something folks shun. Too often we think of holiness—and imagine a Holy God—as confined to the cold austerity of an unheated Puritan meetinghouse rather than cultivated in the hearth-warmed comfort of a mountain chalet.

Yet, in Lewis's judgment: "How little people know who think that holiness is dull. When one meets the real thing (and perhaps, like you, I have met it only once) it is irresistible. If even 10% of the world's population had it, would not the whole world be converted and happy before a year's end?"[8] Rather than rejoice at the very notion of holiness, sinners scheme to ambush and attack it. So, rather like martyrs killed for their goodness, good words often suffer what Lewis called "verbicide," the willful destruction of a word's meaning. He shared the stance of Oliver Wendell Holmes, who said: "Life and language are alike sacred. Homicide and verbicide—that is—violent treatment of a word with fatal results to its legitimate meaning, which is its life—are alike forbidden."[9] Lewis declared: "We cannot stop the verbicides. The most we can do is not to imitate them."[10]

"Apparently," writes Josef Pieper, "the basic words of any language, words that concern the central issues of existence, are particularly subject to perversion."[11] Lewis labeled this tendency to transform good words into their opposite a law: "Give a good quality a name that that name will soon be the name of a defect."[12]

Yet good words, like some endangered species, need preservation. *Holiness* is one of them. Some words—*sin, salvation, honesty, fidelity, Christian, God*—cannot be deleted from our vocabulary any more than some nutrients—calcium, iron, potassium—can be deleted from our diet. For our health's sake, both nutrients and words are necessary. Confucius noted that social reform in a nation begins with the "restoration of names." So, as Lewis wrote: "To save any word from" destruction "is a task worth the efforts of all who love the English language."[13]

We often imagine holiness is embodied in awesome figures like John the Baptist, fiery of eye and hot of tongue, or like an austere Jonathan Edwards, known only to high school and college students for one sermon, "Sinners in the Hands of an Angry God." But Edwards more frequently stressed themes evident in one of his finest books, *Religious Affections.* Therein he declared:

"Holiness, which is the beauty and sweetness of the divine nature, is the proper nature of the Holy Spirit as much as heat is the property of fire, or sweetness is the property of holy anointing oil."[14] Not drabness, but beauty! Not salt for ragged wounds, but healing oil! Such constitute God's holiness.

> ## *The beauty of God's holiness surpasses that of a thousand seaside sunsets or a score of photographic sessions at the Grand Canyon.*

Indeed: the most attractive characteristic of God is His holiness! As David exulted: "Give unto the LORD the glory due unto his name; worship the LORD in the beauty of holiness" (Ps. 29:2, KJV). The beautiful, said one of the greatest Christian theologians, Thomas Aquinas, is "that which pleases upon being seen." When entranced by a beautiful scene, we feel strangely moved, pleased by the sight. Notice how crowds collect to watch the sun as it settles like an iridescent balloon into the ocean, flaming fire across the cloud-freckled sky. Notice cars stop at the Grand Canyon to allow their camera-laden riders to stream to safe viewpoints from which to snap pictures of its grandeur. Rightly seen, the beauty of God's holiness surpasses that of a thousand seaside sunsets or a score of photographic sessions at the Grand Canyon.

Like beauty, sweetness draws us. Birds and bees suck sweet-nectared flowers. Horses trot quickly to take sugar cubes pulled from their trainers' pockets. Children cheerfully consume candy and soft drinks. Never have I seen birds or bees or horses or children forced to eat sweets! So the holiness of God, rightly tasted, attracts us and sweetens every phase of life with its goodness. God's holiness exudes a sweet aroma, tempts our taste buds, and satisfies our sweet tooth.

Throughout his works, C. S. Lewis more frequently mentions

"joy" than "holiness." Yet, rightly understood, the joy he craved comes from the God who is holy; it describes our delight with the wholeness and integrity, the perfection of our being, which is the holiness derived from Him. The "new quality, the bright shadow," that enamored Lewis was a manifestation of ultimate reality. It was, he discovered, "holiness."

And his vision is deeply biblical, for the psalmist declared: "One thing have I desired of the LORD, that will I seek after; that I may dwell in the house of the LORD all the days of my life, to behold the beauty of the LORD, and to inquire in his temple" (Ps. 27:4, KJV).

2 — The Most Beautiful Thing in the World

"A Particular Thing"

If anything is to exist at all, then the Original Thing must be, not a principle nor a generality, much less an "ideal" nor a "value," but an utterly concrete fact.[1]

IF THERE'S A "SHADOW" OF HOLINESS TO ENCOUNTER, there's surely a "holy thing" that casts the shadow. The intimations of holiness come from an ultimately holy One. So, far more than a doctrine to be defined, ultimate "holiness" is a living actuality, a facet of God's being we can encounter and know—just as a man knows his wife's inner beauty that surpasses skin and sinews, clothes and cosmetics. Deeper than a truth to be treasured, holiness resides in the Truing One who aligns and transforms—just as a wise coach's instructions empower an athlete. Consequently, holiness first and last refers to God because it is an inner quality of being basic to His being, something as absolutely imbedded in His person as the gold in the veins of the Sierra Nevada.

All too often discussions of holiness focus on "us men and our salvation" rather than on God. Too often holiness theology and preaching drags in a holy God almost as a caboose-style afterthought, as a means to human holiness. Rather than worshiping the holy One for His goodness and beauty, we try to use Him to make us good and beautiful. But in truth the only real focus for holiness is God, the holy One. Just as good historians should study others, not themselves, so theologians should study God rather than themselves. Thus the Christian faith rightly begins with a wondering adoration of Christ as God's Son, the "exact representation of his being" (Heb. 1:3). In this respect, C. S. Lewis, along with most great Christian thinkers, may be called a holiness theologian, for he continually stressed the absolute holiness of God.

The fact that God is holy is the unfathomable bedrock, the granite foundation that supports the superstructure of Christian faith. In Scripture God simply says, "I am holy." All that we say about Him, all that we understand concerning His will for us, flows from the certainty of that declaration. In the judgment of an influential 20th-century theologian, Gustaf Aulen, we can affirm nothing "about God when it is not projected against the background of his holiness."[2]

Holiness, like love, describes God's nature.

Thomas Oden notes that "holiness is not to be conceived as one trait among many other divine traits. . . . Rather, holiness summarizes, unifies, and integrates all the other incomparably good characteristics of the divine life."[3] R. C. Sproul says, "When the word *holy* is applied to God, it does not single out one single attribute. On the contrary, God is called holy in a general sense. The word is used as a synonym for his deity. That is, the word *holy* calls attention to all that God is."[4] In the Christian tradition, God's many attributes (omnipotence, omniscience, etc.) refer to His powers and acts; but holiness, like love, describes His nature, what He really is.

Plato envisioned reality as ultimately a wholesome fusion of transcendentals such as truth, goodness, and beauty. Countering the relativism of the Sophists, Plato "showed that absolute values exist, that these can be known, and that therefore there is such a thing as truth. He likewise showed that these values are summed up in the majesty of that which we call 'the Good,' and that this good can be realized in the life of man according to the potentialities of each individual."[5] The word Plato coined for God—Agathon/plain—the Good, suggests that "the eternal goodness of God" infuses "moral enlightenment . . . into the soul of the receptive man."[6] Gilbert Meilander notes that "for Plato the goal is nothing less than holiness, likeness to what is good."[7] Now any reading of Lewis reveals his indebtedness to Plato, and I think we can discern a revealing and important correspondence between Plato's transcendentals and Lewis's portrayal of the holiness of God.

In the Old Testament, the word *qodesh*—holiness, that which is separate, set aside—is used hundreds of times. It primarily means that God is uniquely God—utterly unlike all the rival "gods." He is, as Moses learned, "He who Is." His aseity, his underived self-caused existence, undergirds all we say about Him. It's the being-truth toward which all truths point. Only the Creator is the uncreated One. Thus, when we make "graven images," idols of various sorts, we reduce God to disjointed representations of ourselves! We'd like to imagine that we can define Him in human terms, creating Him in our own likeness. Yet God is holy, other-than-us, uniquely God. He is other-than-nature—supernatural! In the words of Isaiah, "'To whom then will you liken Me, or to whom shall I be equal?' says the Holy One" (Isa. 40:25, NKJV). The right response, of course, is "no one!" There is no one at all, nothing in all creation, that rivals the holy One.

When C. S. Lewis tried to explain this, he liked to say that God is a "particular Thing." Something "particular" is one of a kind—a specific event, such as President Lincoln's election in 1860, or a unique work, such as Leonardo da Vinci's *Mona Lisa*. A "thing," of course, has substance, really exists. It stands there like Half Dome in Yosemite National Park. The word *transcendent*—which means "utterly other than, qualitatively different from"—probably best describes this aseity, this facet of His holiness. He is absolutely other than us and our time-and-space world. He is wholly what He is, holy through and through.

Lewis strongly objected to the ways we use slippery words such as *spiritual* and *supernatural,* sucking out their hardness, their substance, as if they were pleasant fictions or escapist daydreams. Rather, he took heavenly realities to be denser, more solid, than earthly ones. As holy—*qodesh*—God stands like the

Rock of Gibraltar amid the ocean swells. As the Source of all beings, God—the ultimate Being—is in fact most substantial, most solid, most immutable. Only a holy God is eternally real. When the resurrected Jesus walked through a wall, it was because He was more solid than stone and simply shoved aside the electrons dancing in their spacious orbits. Just as we walk through water He walked through walls because He was so much denser, so much more solid, than brick and mortar.

> ## As holy, God stands like
> ## the Rock of Gibraltar
> ## amid the ocean swells.

In one of his most intriguing books, *The Great Divorce,* Lewis imagined what might happen if souls in hell had the chance to travel toward heaven. As they unload from the bus and explore the fields that could lead them to heaven, they reveal how far they've fallen into nothingness. They've lost what made them real human beings! They're vapors, wisps of fog drifting about, notably unsolid and anxious to return to hell's isolation. Only redeemed spirits (like George MacDonald, who serves as a guide in the story), have substance, a solidity akin to God's.

So, too, in *Miracles,* Lewis warned against giving God unwarranted "compliments," giving Him shapeless labels such as "infinite" or the "divine milieu"—abstractions that, as Lewis elsewhere quipped, reduce Him to "an infinitely extended rice pudding."[8] Such words tempt us to imagine Him as a formless force or fuzzy energy field of some sort, thus slipping into vague "Star Trek" philosophies. "Let us dare to say," Lewis insisted, "that God is a particular Thing. Once He was the only Thing: but He is creative, He made other things to be. He is not those other things."[9] A holy God cannot be confused with or reduced to what He created, for He is transcendent, utterly other than, His world.

A second meaning of the Hebrew word *qodesh,* holiness, is purity. As a "Particular Thing," a Holy God is not like a piece of laminated wood, the glued-together combination of different materials. He is purely God, through-and-through God. Interlaced with His transcendence, God's purity rightly represents a vital facet of His holiness. Whatever is pure is unadulterated. Pure gold contains no nongold. It's "the real thing." Pure light is nothing but light, and nothing we can do pollutes or alters its nature. Light is wholly, completely light. So God's purity describes His wholeness.

Purity also contains moral dimensions. Pure persons—and God as a person—have moral character. Sexually pure athletes and soldiers attest to their moral character, resisting temptations to betray their spouses. Intellectually pure scholars treasure truth, refusing to misrepresent or distort their findings. Lewis helps us understand that "there are things that God is not" because "He has a determinate character. Thus He is righteous, not a-moral; creative, not inert."[10] Perusing the Old Testament, we find that only one time did God declare "simply I AM, proclaiming the mystery of self-existence. But times without number He says, 'I am the Lord'—I, the ultimate Fact, have this determinate character, and not that."[11] Consequently, Lewis explains, "men are exhorted to 'know the Lord,' to discover and experience this particular character."[12]

You cannot fold impurity into a pure God.

This means that God in His holiness cannot tolerate impurity, sin, dishonesty, moral corruption. The "wrath" of a holy God is part and parcel of His purity. You cannot mix oil and water—and you cannot fold impurity into a pure God. Explaining why, Lewis says, "A God who did not regard this [our sins] with unappeasable distaste would not be a good being. We cannot even wish for such a God—it is like wishing that every nose in the universe were abolished, that smell of hay or roses or the sea should never again delight any creature, because our own breath happens to stink."[13]

A holy God, a pure God, cannot tolerate impurity in His creatures. As Paul warned, "Do you not know that the unrighteous will not inherit the kingdom of God? Do not be deceived; neither the immoral, nor idolaters, nor adulterers, nor sexual perverts, nor thieves, nor the greedy, nor drunkards, nor revilers, nor robbers will inherit the kingdom of God" (1 Cor. 6:9-10, RSV). Just as a good, loving teacher cannot tolerate wrong answers on tests, so God loves us too much to allow us to defile ourselves and His world. Good students want to be shown their errors; they never respect a teacher who excuses their wrong answers in the hopeless task of making them feel good. It follows, then, that "When we merely *say* that we are bad, the 'wrath' of God seems a barbarous doctrine; as soon as we perceive our badness, it appears inevitable, a mere corollary from God's goodness."[14]

Finally, added to transcendence and purity, God's holiness refers to His brilliance—His radiance—the sheer beauty of His being. There is, to use a biblical word often applied to God, a *glory* in His holiness. The Greek word for glory, *doxa,* when used in the Bible, means "a quality belonging to God and is recognized by man only in response to Him." Citing a biblical text, "We give thanks to thee for thy great glory," Lewis added: "He is this glory."[15]

Glory's grandeur shines through significant and watershed biblical passages—Moses on Mount Sinai, Jesus on the Mount of Transfiguration, the Holy Spirit at Pentecost. Glory is like the sun that arises and allows us to turn off the streetlights, to draw back the drapes and read by the light of day. When we see holiness in God, it shines with overpowering luminosity, and we delight in it just as we rejoice at the daily dawn that awakens and uplifts us.

In "The Weight of Glory," one of Lewis's finest essays, he noted that glory "is very prominent in the New Testament and early Christian writings. Salvation is constantly associated with palms, crowns, white robes, thrones, and splendour like the sun and stars."[16] To bask in such royal glory, to hear God say, "Well done, thou good and faithful servant"—is to know the ultimate joy of salvation. For finally "that Face which is the delight or the terror of the universe must be turned upon each of us either with one expression or the other, either conferring glory inexpressible or inflicting shame that can never be cured or disguised."[17]

Before the final Judgment Seat, we will answer to a holy God. To some—in our tolerant, nonjudgmental culture—it seems the big issue is deciding whether or not He has the right to actually judge us! Yet, Lewis insists, "How we think of Him is of no importance except insofar as it is related to how He thinks of us."[18] At the Judgment, we "shall 'stand before' Him, shall appear, shall be inspected. The promise of glory is the promise, almost incredible and only possible by the work of Christ, that some of us, that any of us who really chooses, shall actually survive that examination, shall find approval, shall please God."[19]

Clearly, Lewis held, we are saved by grace through faith. Yet Scripture equally clearly indicates that "without faith it is impossible to please him: for he that cometh to God must believe that he is, and that he is a rewarder of them that diligently seek him" (Heb. 11:6, KJV). Enoch, we're told, "was translated that he should not see death" because in his life "he had this testimony, that he pleased God" (v. 5, KJV). We're urged to "walk worthy of the Lord unto all pleasing" (Col. 1:10, KJV). Paul wrote the Thessalonians, instructing them how "to walk and to please God" (1 Thess. 4:1, KJV).

This holy God, so glorious, so pure, so fully God, will in fact take pleasure in some of His faithful servants. His will, His demands, are not beyond knowing and doing. Thus, for us "to please God . . . to be a real ingredient in the divine happiness . . . to be loved by God, not merely pitied, but delighted in as an artist delights in his work or a father in a son—it seems impossible, a weight or burden of glory which our thoughts can hardly sustain. But so it is."[20]

What Lewis sums up so beautifully was earlier said by Jesus: "Blessed are the pure in heart: for they shall see God" (Matt. 5:8, KJV). The great joy throughout eternity will be to see the truth, goodness, and beauty wrapped up in the Holy Trinity, to know the true happiness—the blessedness—promised to those who rightly serve God.

3 The Fire Forever Burning

"Most Numinous of All"

Instantly—I had been freezing cold till now—a wave of fire passed over me, even down to my numb feet. It was the voice of a god. Who should know better than I? A god's voice had once shattered my whole life. They are not to be mistaken. It may well be that by trickery of priests men have sometimes taken a mortal's voice for a god's. But it will not work the other way. No one who hears a god's voice takes it for a mortal's.
"Lord, who are you?" said I.[1]

YEARS AGO MANY COLLEGIANS' FAVORITE WORD WAS AWESOME. To give ultimate praise to something, they'd call it "totally awesome," voicing their amazement at persons or performances of worth and beauty. What elicited their acclaim, though they'd never have so labeled it, was holiness. When something is all it can be—be it a wide receiver's "circus catch" in a football game or an opera singer's stunning solo—we say it's "awesome," for we're struck by the rightness of its being, the perfection of its nature, the fulfilling of its design.

Lewis endorsed this venerable tradition: we begin to love wisdom when we wonder at the mysteries of existence. We stand in awe—we are awestruck—at the tantalizing questions posed by simply being. Awakening to the beauties of a new day, we sometimes inwardly exclaim: it's just good to be alive; it's delightful just to be! In one of Plato's dialogues, Socrates says:

"Wonder is the feeling of a philosopher, and philosophy begins in wonder."[2] Following Plato, Aristotle concurred: "For it is owing to their wonder that men both now begin and at first began to philosophize."[3]

Yet for all their grandeur, philosophical brews never quench our thirst for meaning. In *The Pilgrim's Regress* (the first "Christian" work written by Lewis), the young wanderer, John, jettisons philosophies that failed to guide him to the alluring "island" he sought. Like John we ultimately crave more than tidy chalkboard sketches, game plans designed in coaches' offices—we want to play and win the game. It's fine to study in school, but most of us want to graduate and then utilize what we've worked to learn. We want something "Other and Outer."[4] We long for things more majestically tangible than mathematical formulae, more gloriously enchanting than syllogistic proofs.

Thus Lewis, eminently rational and gifted in debate, clearheaded and precise in defending the faith, distrusted the kind of rationalism so pervasive in the modern world. It's fine to master computer technology, but it's more satisfying to love and be loved. It's wise to appreciate the grandeur of scientific discoveries, but it's foolish to make "scientism" the guiding spirit of your life.

> *There are magical moments, when we are stunned by the bright shining forth of the divine.*

However useful, Lewis thought "philosophical proofs never, by themselves, lead to religion," for religion is what ushers us into the meaningful realm of reality."[5] He personally found meaning in what Rudolph Otto labeled the experience of the "numinous"—being transfixed like "fans" in the presence of sports or entertainment "celebrities." There are magical moments, for many of us, when we are stunned by the bright shining forth of the divine, feeling what Lewis preferred to call "AWE."[6]

In Lewis's final novel, *Till We Have Faces,* we follow the spiritual journey of Queen Orual, who rages and rebels against the gods. At the end of her life, she wrote a book, detailing her objections, venting her anger. After finishing her treatise, which ended with the words "no answer," she unexpectedly encountered realities beyond description. So she wrote a second short treatise, ending with this confession: "I know now, Lord, why you utter no answer. You are yourself the answer. Before your face questions die away. What other answer would suffice? Only words, words; to be led out to battle against other words."[7] Orual learned the wordless truth of awe, and at the end of her life she bowed before an absolutely awesome One.

Going beyond ourselves, we find the humility to dethrone the tyrannical self from the center of reality; we open ourselves to what transcends us, something greater than the physical world. We bow down and worship the Source of our wonder. We worship when we follow Moses to the "mountain of God" (Exod. 3:1), pause at the burning bush, overwhelmed with *awe* at the presence of the Holy One. In the judgment of Gregory of Nyssa, Moses discerned in the burning bush "the transcendent essence and cause of the universe, on which everything depends, alone subsists."[8] This ancient encounter, this theophany, transformed Moses and enabled him to lead his people to freedom. It also transformed humankind's understanding of God. Following this experience Moses walked in paths suffused with mystery and bathed in the light waves of "glory." The "glory of His presence" is the holiness of His person! Moses was awed by the transcendent goodness of the Holy One.

And that same Holy One shines on those who pause to worship, taking off their shoes to acknowledge His glory. So, Martin Buber wrote: "God says to man as he said to Moses: 'Put off thy shoes from off thy feet'—put off the habitual which encloses your foot and you will recognize that the place on which you happen to be standing at this moment is holy ground. For there is no rung of being on which we cannot find the holiness of God everywhere and at all times."[9] We come to adore Him, Buber said, in "I-Thou" encounters. Lewis, who in the last book he wrote exclaimed "How good Buber is,"[10] shared his view.

To find, on every "rung of being" that "holiness of God everywhere and at all times,"[11] Lewis ever noted the near-at-hand. For we are immersed in His presence. God does not stand on every street corner with a placard declaring "Here I Am." He doesn't announce each morning from a million loudspeakers atop soaring skyscrapers that HE IS LORD. So we, too, rarely recognize Him, thinking He only appears in mountaintop epiphanies. Yet, as Lewis so wisely wrote, "in order to find God it is perhaps not always necessary to leave the creatures behind. We may ignore, but we can nowhere evade, the presence of God. The world is crowded with Him. He walks everywhere incognito. And the incognito is not always hard to penetrate. The real labor is to remember, to attend. In fact, to come awake. Still more, to remain awake."[12]

> *Dream-walking through life, many of us fail to sense the divine surrounding us.*

This is because, he continued: "There is here no question of a God 'up there' or 'out there'; rather the present operation of God 'in here,' as the ground of my own being, and God 'in there,' as the ground of the matter that surrounds me, and God embracing and uniting both in the daily miracle of finite consciousness."[13]

Living in darkened caves, blinded by fear, dream-walking through life, many of us fail to sense the divine surrounding us. Yet there's hope! As Lewis insists, God pervades His world with His wondrous presence. What we need do is wake up, look around, note carefully what is real, and allow it to direct our mind to what is really real. When we do so, we pray! In prayer, and in I-Thou encounters, we come to know the Holy One. "Now the moment of prayer," Lewis said, "is for me—or involves for me as its condition—the awareness, the re-awakened awareness that this 'real world' and 'real self' are very far from being rock-bottom realities."[14] Prayer attunes us to what is really real!

In prayer, we seek to be real and to know the Real One. "The prayer preceding all prayers is 'May it be the real I who speaks. May it be the real Thou that I speak to.'"[15] Such is the possibility of prayer that there is "at every moment, a possible theophany.

Here is the holy ground; the Bush is burning now."[16] So, Paul urged, "Pray without ceasing" (1 Thess. 5:17, KJV). Rightly praying enables us to enter into the spirit of the psalmist: "Bless the LORD, O my soul: and all that is within me, bless his holy name. Bless the LORD, O my soul, and forget not all his benefits: who forgiveth all thine iniquities; who healeth all thy diseases; who redeemeth thy life from destruction; who crowneth thee with lovingkindness and tender mercies; who satisfieth thy mouth with good things; so that thy youth is renewed like the eagle's" (Ps. 103:1-5, KJV).

PART TWO

GOD'S HOLY TEMPLE
"GLORIOUS AND EXCELLENT"
BY DESIGN

4   A Mind like the Mind of the Maker

"A Shadow of an Image"

We were made to be neither cerebral men nor visceral men, but Men. Not beasts nor angels but Men—things at once rational and animal.[1]

He wants each man, in the long run, to be able to recognize all creatures (even himself) as glorious and excellent things.[2]

MORE THAN A CENTURY AGO one of Europe's most brilliant philosophers sat on a bench in a park in Frankfurt, Germany. He wore shabby clothes and looked like a scruffy tramp. Concerned to keep the park clear of vagrants and riffraff, a groundskeeper confronted him, demanding: "Who are you?" In response Arthur Schopenhauer replied: "I wish to God I knew."

"I wish to God I knew." Schopenhauer spoke for sinful man. And his casual reference to God reveals a critical truth: not knowing God, we do not know who we are. As Peter Kreeft, a contemporary American philosopher, insists: "You can't even know yourself by yourself. The self is a *koan,* a puzzle that is unsolvable in principle—like 'tell me the somebody you were when you were nobody.' *Only God can know you.* The secret of your identity is in your Author alone because you are his character."[3] Our century, with all its confusions—haunted by phrases such as "the death of God" or "the death of the soul"—could easily be labeled the "Age of Schopenhauer." (Interestingly enough, as a youngster C. S. Lewis was deeply influenced by Schopenhauer's brooding pessimism, which permeates many

of his early poems.) Though less moody and morose than Schopenhauer, many of us wonder in our somber moments who we really are. We're usually comfortable talking about what we like to eat or wear, about our job, about our towns and teams. But the really important question is this: Who are we, really? When we don't know, resorting to social "games" or aimless diversions, we tacitly confess to our confusion. To the extent we're unreal, it's because we've lost the holiness that makes us whole. Conversely, the joy and peace that accompany being real ultimately flow from a wholeness of being that is derived from God.

Addressing this question, C. S. Lewis linked hands with a host of Christian thinkers, declaring: I am a beloved person, rational and free, created in the "image of God." Despite our many failures, there are remnants of a lost majesty, a shadowy grandeur to us! Certainly newspaper headlines magnify and sensationalize the most depraved human activities, and our attention often exclusively locks, like a laser beam, on our own faults, our own sinfulness. But such must never obscure for us God's first and final design: we are made to be holy as He is holy. As such, there's much beauty and purity to human nature. Ultimately all goodness, of course, comes from a good God. All holiness resides in a holy God and flowers only so long as it remains rooted in Him, flowing like a spring from His transcendent goodness and glory. All creatures, great and small, reveal and participate in His holiness, so there's a grandeur to humankind's original design, a durable dignity in human nature.

We believe this because, as Thomas Aquinas said, created "things were produced by God in a supremely excellent way; for the most perfect Being does everything in the most perfect way."[4] As a popular mantra puts it: "God made me. And God don't make no junk!" Absolutely good, God made all creatures so that, when following their God-given inclinations, they seek what's good; and "all good is a certain imitation of the supreme Good, just as all being is a certain imitation of the first Being. Therefore the movements and actions of all things tend toward assimilation with the divine goodness."[5]

Holiness advocates, unlike Christians of a more pessimistic cast, neither despise the created essence nor abandon hope for the final perfection of humankind. There is, especially in the Eastern Orthodox and Wesleyan traditions, an "optimism of grace," which gives them a cheerful countenance. Yes, we're sinners. Yes, we do much evil. But despite it all, there persists a fundamental goodness to human nature that can be wrested from the claws of evil, cleansed and transformed into the very likeness of Christ Jesus.

> *There are no ordinary people.*
> *You have never talked to*
> *a mere mortal.*

Admittedly, like a plane in flight heading toward the wrong destination, we need correction, rerouting. Admittedly, like cardiovascular patients, we need medical attention and radical surgery to restore us to health. But while honestly admitting the reality of sin, holiness theology forever celebrates the primary and potential grandeur of humankind. In one of Lewis's Narnian stories, *Prince Caspian,* there's a passage where Aslan crowns young Caspian and commissions him to rule Narnia. This reveals Lewis's understanding of man's paradoxical brilliance and blight:

> "Do you mark all this well, King Caspian?"
>
> "I do indeed, Sir," said Caspian. "I was wishing that I came of a more noble lineage."
>
> "You come of the Lord Adam and the Lady Eve," said Aslan. "And that is both honour enough to erect the head of the poorest beggar, and shame enough to bow the shoulders of the greatest emperor in earth. Be content."[6]

There's nobility in our ancestry! Genealogical research, if it goes back far enough, cannot but make us proud! Better than finding dukes and barons in our family tree, we find a divine Designer's imprint in our genes. By nature, each of us really is somebody. In fact, Lewis insisted: "There are no ordinary people. You have never talked to a mere mortal."[7] Sometimes, when we feel good about ourselves or our family or friends, we're right! It's not pride, but an honest apprehension of divine truth, laced into the very eyelets of our being. This awareness reminds us of where we have come from and where we are bound. The Bible tells us we're created in the very image of God! More importantly, we must look reverently at those around us, for we're surrounded by "possible gods and goddesses," and even the least impressive of folks "may one day be a creature which, if you say it now, you would be strongly tempted to worship, or else a horror and a corruption such as you now meet, if at all, only in a nightmare."[8]

Reflecting on human nature, beholding the grandeur of our design, engages us in a "holy" kind of thinking that sees as God sees, and thus enables us to focus on what's truly other than ourselves. We then follow truths that lead us to objective realities. Similarly, when we think logically we look away from ourselves, search for the Logos, come to conclusions without imposing our own preferences, and seek truth in things other than our own desires. Truly rational thought elevates our minds, lifting them toward higher truths. Thus our true dignity, that which makes us truly man, is our mind. In Aquinas' view, "The most excellent creatures are intellectual. Indeed they are said to be fashioned in God's image for the very reason that among all creatures they approach most clearly to likeness with God."[9]

Explaining the thought of Thomas Aquinas, which on this score seems similar to Lewis's, Josef Pieper says we're able to know things because they have design. Without some form, shapeless "stuff," like Silly Putty, cannot be defined or grasped. But as we learn in John's Gospel, all things are formed by the Logos of God—all that is was created by a rational God. So we can rationally understand them: "Because things come forth from the eye of God, they partake wholly of the nature of the Logos, that is, they are lucid and limpid to their very depths. It is their origin in the Logos which makes them knowable to men."[10]

Lewis always insisted that living well—holiness—requires an enlightened mind!

To the extent we see as God sees (though admittedly "through a glass, darkly"), and insofar as we conform our minds to the mind of God, the reality of His Being, we enter into and know by His holiness. As Lewis noted: "For the wise men of old the cardinal problem had been how to conform the soul to reality, and the solution had been knowledge, self-discipline, and virtue."[11] One of those "wise men of old" for Lewis was Plato, who, in "Theaetetus," has Socrates say that we're called to "become like the divine so far as we can."[12] Like Augustine, Lewis was in many ways a "Christian Platonist," and he urges us to escape the cavelike darkness of ignorance and strive to come to "the Good," to know what is real, to expose our souls, like wax to a seal, to the divine stamp. To Plato, becoming good, participating in "Agathon"—ultimate goodness—is the goal of life. And that goal, he makes clear, is a holiness that comes to us on an intellectual level. Concurring, Lewis always insisted that living well—holiness—requires an enlightened mind!

Of all the world's wonders, the human mind is a wonder to behold! If you look at a brain in a laboratory, it looks like a three pound glob of gray mush. As Ashley Brilliant, a contemporary cartoonist, quips, "Whatever else you may say about it, it is definitely more intelligent than it looks."[13] In fact, your mind's one of the most impressive organisms in the entire universe. In Lewis's words: "Men look on the starry heavens with reverence: monkeys do not. The silence of the eternal spaces terrified Pascal, but it was the greatness of Pascal that enabled them to do so. When we are frightened by the greatness of the universe, we are almost literally frightened by our own shadows: . . . I do not say we are wrong to tremble at his shadow; it is a shadow of an image of God."[14]

So nothing better illustrates the "image of God" in us than our ability to reason. Thinking gives us a unique dignity. Unlike other animals, Lewis wrote, man "wants to know things, wants to find out what reality is like, simply for the sake of knowing. When that desire is completely quenched in anyone, I think he has become something less than human."[15]

While we lost much of our original wholeness in the Fall, we're still able to think logically. Ignorance certainly stalks us, as silent and stealthy as hypertension. Mental laziness certainly tugs at us, sucking us down into the quicksand of jargon and second-hand opinions. Propaganda, skillfully deployed by the forces of ads and fads, certainly encircles and chokes us with the enervating suction of a vacuum chamber. Yet, for all that, we can follow syllogistic arguments (e.g., if man is mortal and Socrates is a man, then Socrates is mortal). We can find geometric demonstrations persuasive: the Pythagorean theorem never fails! We acknowledge powerful natural hungers that persuade us that things designed to satisfy them must be real: God, immortality, freedom, justice. While never infallible, our mind meshes with the infallible mind of God when we think rightly. In a poem, "Reason," Lewis wrote:

> Set on the soul's acropolis the reason stands
> A virgin, arm'd, commercing with celestial light,
> And he who sins against her has defiled his own
> Virginity: no cleansing makes his garment white;
> So clear is reason.[16]

In his apologetic works, artful books that led some to label him the "apostle to the agnostics," Lewis skillfully assembled evidence and utilized logic, following "reason," this uniquely human ability to think. Thought's eternal worth is highlighted by the regularity with which dictatorial regimes seek to suppress it. Before killing people, antihuman principalities and powers destroy free speech and try to stamp out independent thought. Determined to thwart our reason, demonic forces deploy slogans and distribute misinformation. They deal in lies and illogic like casino cards. In fact, Satan (like Screwtape in *The Screwtape Letters*) seeks to mislead us, as he did the young man assigned to the tempter Wormwood, by immersing us in "jargon, not argument, [which] is the best way to keep him out of the Church"[17]—or, we must add, out of God's eternal kingdom.

The antireason foes opposed by Lewis 40 years ago, in works such as *The Screwtape Letters* and *The Abolition of Man*, have been vividly victorious in our century. As a teacher, Lewis cared about education, and his writings sought to address youngsters' needs and temptations. He realized the power of sin to turn children away from the truth, to suck them into joining Satan's camp. Despite Lewis's efforts, however, Satan's strategies have scored spectacular successes, especially in a culture influenced by what's often called "postmodernism," where reason is routinely dismissed and despised.

That such attitudes are rampant is evident in recent books focusing on young people, such as *Jesus for a New Generation: Putting the Gospel in the Language of Xers*. Too often unchallenged in school and unsupervised at home, many youngsters turn to TV as a "surrogate parent,"[18] which teaches them to live for the moment, embracing Nike's "just do it" philosophy. "Life is short. Play hard." Such "media saturation," pulsating with booming rock music and dancing with images on the screen, leaves kids "little time for reflection. We don't like to spend time thinking and reflecting, because most of the things we have to think about are unpleasant—and even scary."[19] Consequently, as novelist Walker Percy wisely noted, "'This is not the Age of Enlightenment but the Age of Not Knowing What to Do.'"[20] Or, as a Bud Dry beer ad urges: "Why ask why?"

When we follow such advice, when we refuse to ask *why*, we fail to think. Thus today many of us rely far more on feelings than on thought. Folks who "feel" have difficulty thinking logically. In Kevin Ford's judgment, "My peers have no fundamental starting points for thinking linearly and logically about God, about reality, about their own meaning and place in the universe."[21] Thus, in Christian churches, traditionally intellectual approaches—teaching doctrine, demonstrating the illogic of heresies—fail to reach Generation X.

From a different perspective, Peter Sacks has published *Generation X Goes to College: An Eye-Opening Account of Teaching in Postmodern America*. Trying to explain what's wrong with much of higher education, Sacks tackles postmodernism's "revolt against reason and thoughtfulness."[22] Modernity, with its confidence in reason, may well be dying! Sacks' students, their values and behaviors, illustrated the impact of a "profound cultural revolt that has occurred in Western, postindustrial societies," and may be "aptly called the Postmodern Generation."[23]

Slogans culled from popular culture define it: "Anything goes" indicates postmodernity's distaste for rules and authorities. "Question Authority" justifies everyone questioning everything. "Authorities" rarely rule. "Trust No One," says *The X-Files,* a popular TV show. "Here we are now/Entertain us," a musical lyric, leads Sacks to suggest that we update Descartes' famous axiom to read "I am entertained, therefore I am."[24] So neither truth nor reality, logic nor history, have substance. Just as Hollywood's filmmakers project whatever "realities" they want on the screen, so postmodern academics insist nothing "real" exists beyond our own visions and fabrications. Reality is nothing but a "construct," be it individual or social, and truth is simply the opinion that best enables us to negotiate the momentary situation.

To an alarming extent Generation X illustrates Aldus Huxley's *Brave New World,* "whose inhabitants had repudiated thinking and reflection for the constant desire to be amused."[25] Indeed, we're *Amusing Ourselves to Death,* according to an educator, Neal Postman. So many students never learn to think. "When you've grown up locked on to the spectacle, notions of truth, reality, and substance recede into meaninglessness. What is meaningful is what is momentarily before your eyes."[26]

To be fully human,
we must think rationally.

Were C. S. Lewis alive, he'd not be surprised at today's hostility to reason, for it's an outgrowth of educational trends clearly evident in his lifetime. The *Abolition of Man,* written in the 1940s, perceptively predicted what would come when educators failed to train youngsters how to think rightly. Yet he would, I believe, continue to uphold both the dignity of man and rationality. To be fully human, we must think rationally. To argue, to reason rightly, we assume the validity of certainties of logical laws that, like the speed of light, never change.

So we "must begin by admitting the self-evidence of logical thought and then believe all other things only in so far as they agree with that. The validity of thought is central: all other things have to be fitted in round it as best they can."[27] Consequently: "If the feeling of certainty which we express by words like must be and therefore and since is a real perception of how things outside our own minds really 'must' be, well and good.

But if this certainty is merely a feeling in our own minds and not a genuine insight into realities beyond them—if it merely represents the ways our minds happen to work—then we can have no knowledge. Unless human reasoning is valid nothing can be true."[28]

> *To see ourselves as "glorious and excellent things" is to see the image of God still lingering in our mind.*

If my reason rightly discerns truth, it must be aligned with a reason that is basic to reality, a rationality that explains the rational workings of the cosmos. Ultimately, as Lewis says in *Mere Christianity*, God's ways make sense—even when we disagree with them, for: "He is the source from which all your reasoning power comes: you could not be right and He wrong any more than a stream can rise higher than its own source. When you are arguing against Him you are arguing against the very power that makes you able to argue at all: it is like cutting off the branch you are sitting on."[29]

To see ourselves as "glorious and excellent things"[30] is to see the image of God still lingering in our mind, often as a "shadow" reminding us of our lost grandeur. "What is man," I wonder, "that thou art mindful of him, and the son of man that thou dost care for him?" Then I'm told, by Holy Scripture: "thou hast made him little less than God, and dost crown him with glory and honor" (Ps. 8:4-5, RSV). Then "I will praise thee; for I am fearfully and wonderfully made" (139:14, KJV).

5 A Will Still Free to Will God's Will

"The Modus Operandi of Destiny"

He cannot ravish. He can only woo.[1]

Free will is the modus operandi of destiny.[2]

IN PERELANDRA *(THE SECOND VOLUME OF HIS ENCHANTING SPACE TRILOGY)*, C. S. Lewis portrays Professor Elwin Ransom's journey to Venus, a newly created planet, where he participates in a story much like the biblical account of Adam and Eve in the Garden of Eden. Placed thereon by the Creator, Maleldil, and entrusted with the planet's destiny, we find a queen, the "Green Lady," and a king. They illustrate God's original design. Ransom journeys to Perelandra in a magical space casket and meets the Green Lady. Soon thereafter, the evil physicist Weston (Ransom's antagonist in the first volume, *Out of the Silent Planet)*, arrives and seeks to get the Green Lady to defy her Maker, to set her own sail and determine her own destiny on Perelandra.

In this story, as Thomas Howard writes, we encounter, like a friend's oft-told story, a familiar theme: "the old theme of human freedom, choice, goodness, the Will of God, and of how these all harmonize in any sort of pattern."[3] Gliding like an Olympic ice skater in the narrative's spotlight, the Green Lady struggles with temptation. Were she not free, of course, there'd be no struggle. There's never a struggle when a straitjacket has been firmly laced up, nor when the iron door of a maximum security cell has clanged shut.

Ransom, too, freely engages in the struggle with Weston. He seeks to speak God's Word and carry out His assignment. He does battle—ultimately resorting to bloody, hand-to-hand physical combat—with Satan's emissary, Weston, the Un-man. In the midst of his very physical battle, Ransom suddenly realized: "Thus, and not otherwise, the world was made. Either something or nothing must depend on individual choices. And if something, who could set bounds to it? A stone may determine the course of a river. He was that stone at this horrible moment which had become the centre of the whole universe. The eldila of all worlds, the sinless organisms of everlasting light, were silent in Deep Heaven to see what Elwin Ransom of Cambridge would do."[4]

> *One of the glowing vestiges of God's image still evident in man, shining like a house light on a darkened porch, is his free will.*

Added to the mind with its remarkable ability to reason, one of the glowing vestiges of God's image still evident in man, shining like a house light on a darkened porch, is his free will. The fact that he reasons entails man's "freedom of choice." As Thomas Aquinas explains: "The intellect does not act or desire without forming a judgment, as lifeless beings do, nor is the judgment of the intellect the product of natural impulses, as in brutes, but results from a true apprehension of the object."[5]

When Screwtape instructed Wormwood, in *The Screwtape Letters,* he wrote: "Think of your man as a series of concentric circles, his will being the innermost, his intellect coming next, and finally his fantasy. You can hardly hope, at once, to exclude from all the circles everything that smells of the Enemy: but you must keep on shoving all the virtues outward till they are finally located in the circle of fantasy, and all the desirable qualities inward into the Will. It is only in so far as they reach the will and are there embodied in habits that the virtues are really fatal to us."[6]

In our will, what Scripture generally calls "the heart," we freely make eternal decisions. Not everyone, of course, shares

Lewis's belief in such free will. An influential journalist in Lewis's youth, Robert Blatchford, declared: "Before we can propagate our religion of Determinism and Humanism, we must first clear the ground of Free Will, of sin against God, and the belief in the divine inspiration of the Bible."[7] Decades later, an American behaviorist, B. F. Skinner, specifically attacked Lewis (by name) twice in his best-selling treatise, *Beyond Freedom and Dignity,* an all-out assault on the very possibility of free will and responsible behavior.

Century after century, such thinkers have discounted the very possibility of human freedom. Denying it—then collapsing into comfortable hammocks of indolence or inviting the protective canopy of tyranny—frees us from responsibility for our actions. Thus we can blame others, or our environment, or God, for our failures. If our actions are determined by the stars, as astrologists argue, or by environmental stimuli, as behavioristic criminologists or welfare workers insist, we need never take responsibility for our actions.

The same issue, determinism or free will, has provoked endless discussion in Christian circles as well. Clearly biblical themes—predestination, free choice, God's call to all—cannot easily be reconciled. The classic text, Rom. 8:28-30, expresses the whole issue: "And we know that all things work together for good to those who love God, to those who are the called according to His purpose. For whom He foreknew, He also predestined to be conformed to the image of His Son, that He might be the firstborn among many brethren. Moreover whom He predestined, these He also called; whom He called, these He also justified; and whom He justified, these He also glorified" (NKJV).

A balanced perspective is notoriously difficult to attain. Masterful theologians such as Augustine can be quoted on both sides! A careful study of Augustine, however, finds him saying: "Let us take care not to defend grace in such a way that we would seem to take away free choice; nor again can we insist so strongly on free choice that we could be judged in our proud impiety, ungrateful for the grace of God."[8]

Yet some theologians, influenced by Martin Luther and John Calvin, have so celebrated God's grace as to minimize or deny man's free role in cooperating with His saving work. Luther, for example, early in his life wrote a treatise, "The Bondage of the Will," absolutely denying any free will. Toward the end of his life, he asserted that it was one of few things he had written that he treasured. "Luther calls the issue of free will the 'res ipsa summa causae' ('the most important aspect of the matter') and the 'cardo rerum' ('the hinge on which all turns')."[9] Similarly, John Calvin insisted that in the act of saving faith Christ "seized" the believer, and that, consequently, "eternal life is foreordained for some, and eternal damnation for others."[10] Such "eternal and immutable" judgments, whereby God saves some and damns others, are solely God's to make. In this free will denying tradition, it logically follows, one's growth in grace, all holiness of heart and life, derives solely from God.

Yet other theologians, swimming with the powerful mainstream of the ancient and medieval theological tradition, have followed the Cappadocian Fathers (Basil, Gregory of Nazianzus, Gregory of Nyssa), James Arminius, John Wesley, and C. S. Lewis. They insist that salvation is solely God's to give, but unless we freely choose to follow Him, there is no reason to preach and teach and urge men to respond to the gospel. Indeed there is strong support for proclaiming the transforming, sanctifying possibilities of grace in this tradition.

> *Hidden in our hearts there's a*
> *liberty bell that rings,*
> *calling us to live in accord*
> *with our Designer's blueprint.*

Though Lewis disliked theological disputes, the issue of free will was sufficiently momentous to prod him to enter this fray, where he clearly sided with the free will advocates. He could not comprehend a loving God who wanted "automata" rather than children, and he could construct no formula for ethics that deleted human responsibility from the equation. As he said, "God has made it a rule for Himself that He won't alter people's character by force. He can and will alter them—but only if the people will let Him."[11]

Deep down within the well of our heart there's a sigh for freedom. Like wind chimes softly stroked by the wind, we're attuned to liberty's breeze. Hidden in our hearts there's a liberty bell that rings, again and again, calling us to live in accord with our Designer's blueprint. And most of us feel that we are, as human beings, not only designed to be free but also capable of acting freely. We hold others responsible when they mistreat us, and we especially resent tyrants' schemes to reduce us to slavery, to rip away our personal freedom. We claim, on a daily basis, that ancient birthright, granted Adam and Eve in the Garden of Eden: "You are free" (Gen. 2:16).

> *Freedom and love are Siamese twins. You can't cut them apart without killing them both.*

But, strangely enough, we often fail to live freely. In truth, it's hard to be free! Amid all our celebrations acclaiming "freedom," most of us confess, with Will Rogers, that "liberty doesn't work as well in practice as it does in speeches." In part the difficulty comes from confusing two legitimate kinds of "freedom." There's a freedom from others—the freedom adolescents want when fleeing parental control. Then there's a freedom to be ourselves—the freedom of a polished jazz pianist improvising on a score. "To know how to free oneself is nothing; the arduous thing is to know what to do with one's freedom," wrote Andre Gide.[12]

Adam and Eve chose to be free from God, escaping His rules and rule. They easily slipped away from their covenant with God, but they found it difficult to survive well on their own. In gaining freedom from God's rule they lost the freedom to be godlike, the freedom an adult son enjoys while working alongside his father on the family farm. Adam and Eve chose freedom from the assignment to "tend the garden" and lost the freedom to live at ease in paradise, relaxing at home as God's children in His world.

Thus, Lewis asserted, "Man is now a horror to God and to

himself and a creature ill-adapted to the universe not because God made him so but because he has made himself so by the abuse of his free will."[13] The quest to be free from things—unfettered by others, obligations, oaths—proves largely illusory. For the only true freedom is the freedom to be what we're designed to be, to become lovers freely giving ourselves away. Freedom and love are Siamese twins. You can't cut them apart without killing them both. Thus lovers wanting love grant others freedom. Love must be free or it cannot be.

Above all, freedom in love demands faithfulness to the beloved. As Albert Camus said, "Freedom is nothing but the chance to be better."[14] "You are free," God said to Adam and Eve, "free to eat from any tree." They had the choice, and they freely chose to eat from the wrong tree. This biblical understanding undergirds one of C. S. Lewis's most profound insights, summed up nicely in *Mere Christianity:* "God created things which had free will. That means creatures which can go either wrong or right. Some people think they can imagine a creature which was free but had no possibility of going wrong; I cannot. If a thing is free to be good it is also free to be bad. And free will is what has made evil possible. Why, then, did God give them free will? Because free will, though it makes evil possible, is also the only thing that makes possible any love or goodness or joy worth having."[15]

Making us free was all Love could do! In God's initial plan, loving activities, freely pursued, would establish paradise. Such freedom is striking on the planet Malacandra, the planet Ransom explored in *Out of the Silent Planet* (the first volume of Lewis's space trilogy). Here one encounters strange creatures— hrossa, sorns, pfifltriggs—who cheerfully accept their creaturely assignments and joyfully live according to their divine design. When Ransom told them about life on earth, they could hardly comprehend such things as "war, slavery, and prostitution." Seeking an explanation, one suggested that earth—the "Silent Planet"—must lack a ruler, a counterpart to Malacandra's Oyarsa. Indeed, we learn:

> **"It is because every one of them wants to be a little Oyarsa himself," said Augray.**

"They cannot help it," said the old sorn. "There must be rule, yet how can creatures rule themselves? Beasts must be ruled by hnau and hnau by eldila and eldila by Maleldil. These creatures have no eldila. They are like one trying to lift himself by his own hair—or one trying to see over a whole country when he is on a level with it—like a female trying to beget young on herself."[16]

Similarly, in *The Screwtape Letters,* Uncle Screwtape admitted, in a letter to his nephew, Wormwood: "One must face the fact that all the talk about His love for men, and His service being perfect freedom, is not (as one would gladly believe) mere propaganda, but an appalling truth. He really *does* want to fill the universe with a lot of loathsome little replicas of Himself— creatures whose life, on its miniature scale, will be qualitatively like His own, not because He has absorbed them but because their wills freely conform to His."[17]

Accordingly, Lewis argued, so far as we can understand: "A world of automata—of creatures that worked like machines— would hardly be worth creating. The happiness which God designs for His higher creatures is the happiness of being freely, voluntarily united to Him and to each other in an ecstasy of love and delight compared with which the most rapturous love between a man and a woman on this earth is mere milk and water. And for that they must be free."[18]

Yet to live freely involves accepting responsibility—something we'd usually rather avoid! We often prefer to define "freedom" as limitless self-will. Modern Americans, Judge Robert Bork insists, in *Slouching Towards Gomorrah,* are thus addicted to an "autonomous individualism" that is dissolving the nation. Accepting responsibility means freely recognizing limits, respecting those boundaries. This defines us as creatures.

It also involves responding to God's offer to restore us to our lost standing, our lost holiness. As Lewis explained: "Creatures are made in their varying ways images of God without their own collaboration or even consent. It is not so that they become sons of God."[19] This comes about through the union of wills—our will with God's will. We choose to follow Jesus! Imitating Him, "Our model is the Jesus, not only of Calvary, but of the workshop, the roads, the crowds, the clamorous demands and surly oppositions, the lack of all peace and privacy, the interruptions."[20]

When he was asked to give a series of talks on the Christian faith for the British Broadcasting Company in 1941, Lewis decided to focus on "The Law of Nature, or Objective Right and Wrong," trying to lay a groundwork for evangelism. "It seems to me," he wrote, "that the New Testament, by preaching repentance and forgiveness, always assumes an audience who already believe in the Law of Nature and know they have disobeyed it."[21] Since many moderns have tossed aside the "Natural Law's" certitudes, he thought it necessary to demonstrate its truth so hearers could perhaps recover some "sense of guilt."[22] Before believing in One who saves from sin we need to believe in sin! Before celebrating grace we must confess our failure to live the law!

Lewis always believed that by nature we can understand basic moral truth and admit its rightness. Along with our ability to think rationally, we have the capacity to recognize goodness. Part of man's grandeur is his capacity to see the moral law, the natural law inscribed in his nature. We know how we should live. Just notice, he suggests, the next time you observe two people arguing. That they argue shows they both assume there is something right and something wrong. Consequently "human beings, all over the earth, have this curious idea that they ought to behave in a certain way, and cannot really get rid of it."[23]

Knowing how we should live and actually living that way, are, of course, demonstrably different issues. We are, all too frequently, reminded of the moral law's truth immediately after breaking it. We feel guilty: guilt for failure, guilt for transgressing known moral laws, guilt for doing what we don't want others to do, guilt for sinning. As Lewis says, "No man knows how bad he is till he has tried very hard to be good."[24] If we feel guilt for failures, we know we could have acted differently. We are free to do what's right or wrong. However bent toward evil we may be, we retain enough of our original goodness to freely choose good or evil. Without the freedom to respond, without the possibility to live righteously, there's no sense to the commandment "Ye shall be holy: for I the LORD your God am holy" (Lev. 19:2, KJV).

But Lewis insisted that we are in fact free. Here he joined scores of Orthodox thinkers, such as Irenaeus of Lyons, a second-century theologian, who wrote: "The expression, 'How often would I have gathered thy children together and thou wouldst not,' set forth the ancient law of human liberty, because God made man a free (agent) from the beginning, possessing his own soul to obey the behests of God voluntarily, and not by compulsion of God. For there is no coercion with God, but a good will (toward us) is present with Him continually."[25]

Similarly, in Ecclesiasticus 15:11-20 (RSV), we read:

Do not say, "Because of the Lord I left the right way"; for he will not do what he hates. Do not say, "It was he who led me astray"; for he has no need of a sinful man. The Lord hates all abominations, and they are not loved by those who fear him. It was he who created man in the beginning, and he left him in the power of his own inclination. If you will, you can keep the commandments, and to act faithfully is a matter of your own choice. He has placed before you fire and water: stretch out your hand for whichever you wish. Before a man are life and death, and whichever he chooses will be given to him. For great is the wisdom of the Lord; he is mighty in power and sees everything; his eyes are on those who fear him, and he knows every deed of man. He has not commanded any one to be ungodly, and he has not given any one permission to sin.

PART THREE

A MOST UNGODLY
"BENT TOWARD EVIL"

6 We're Vandals, All of Us

"All Sin Is Sacrilege"

*Hence all sin, whatever else it is,
is a form of sacrilege.*[1]

IN THE FILM GRAND CANYON, *A TOW TRUCK DRIVER LECTURED* the leader of a group of young hoodlums who were harassing his customer, whose car had broken down. Their behavior distressed him. "Man," he said to one of them, "the world ain't supposed to work like this. Maybe you don't know that, but this ain't the way it's supposed to be. I'm supposed to be able to do my job without askin' you if I can. And that dude is supposed to be able to wait with his car without you rippin' him off. Everything's supposed to be different than what it is here."[2]

Anguished phrases such as "this ain't the way it's supposed to be" or "that's not fair," remind us of truths even some modern Christians (immersed in therapeutic quests for self-esteem) too easily ignore. Pretending all's well, declaring we're all OK, asserting the world's getting better and better, may divert our attention for a season, but we cannot forever evade the darker truths about human nature. Photographic observers, recording things as they are, cannot but protest the damning impact of modernity's denial of the reality of sin.

Skilled propagandists have applied a plaster sheen—a glistening coat of humanistic whitewash—on society's inner tombs of death and decay. With stereos roaring and jet planes tearing through the skies, we're numbed to reality. Whether astutely "surfing the web" on our computer or twirling a casino's roulette wheel, we're dying inside and conspire to silence any words of truth that would indict us. As surely as defendants in high profile criminal trials, we blind ourselves to the evidence and pretend we are innocent until the end. Yet when even toughened tow truck drivers exclaim that "everything's supposed to be different than what it is here," we can no longer evade the fact that our world needs an awakened awareness of sin.

In her introduction to one edition of Lewis's *The Screwtape Letters,* an American poet, Phyllis McGinley, perceptively wrote:

> **Of all losses man has sustained in the past hundred years, no deprivation has been so terrible as the abandonment of private guilt. It was dreadful for him to lose a Creator. It was worse than dreadful, it was shattering, for him to cast off responsibility. When society substituted shame for guilt, it amputated half of the human psyche. Animals can feel shame. Only man can know that he is guilty of a sin. The splendid, consoling thing about sin is that it implies forgiveness. One who has done wrong can be sorry and recover.**[3]

Intent on substituting shame for guilt, therapists of various sorts have sought to relabel moral faults, treating them as diseases. So killers kill because they're "sick," infected by a "sick society." Child abusers abuse because they've been abused and developed an abusive syndrome. Yet, McGinley argues: "To call sin a sickness is the devil's cruelest modern weapon. Self-respect rests on a basis of free will, and to make our transgressions—and therefore our virtues—involuntary is an act which Screwtape himself must have helped to incite."[4]

"To make our transgressions— and therefore our virtues— involuntary is an act which Screwtape himself must have helped to incite."

C. S. Lewis tried, in works such as *The Screwtape Letters,* to do this in the 1940s, and his words easily guide us to a fresh yet thoroughly traditional understanding of sin's damning power. Most of his works include references to, if not analyses of, the pervasive power of evil on planet earth. Carried away with the avalanche of modernity's lost awareness of God, the consciousness of sin has been buried under the debris of socialistic utopias and psychological denials. We've devised effective ways, sleight-of-hand magical tricks, to blind ourselves to truths earlier generations found overwhelmingly self-evident. It's easily done. Just follow this prescription: "Avoid silence, avoid solitude, avoid any train of thought that leads off the beaten track. Concentrate on money, sex, status, health and (above all) on your own grievances. Keep the radio on. Live in a crowd. Use plenty of sedation. If you must read books, select them very carefully. But you'd be safer to stick to the papers."[5]

Thus some of Lewis's most insightful analyses update the thought of John Milton and Augustine, whose versions of the Fall represent the teaching of the Church as a whole. This means, first, as Augustine taught: "God created all things without exception good, and because they are good, 'No Nature (i.e. no positive reality) is bad and the word Bad denotes merely privation of good.'"[6] When God labeled all He made "good," He revealed to us the fact that parsnips and planets, mice and men, have been blessed by His matchless touch. When God made eyes that see He made something good, however we may use or abuse them.

Second, Lewis embraces another of Augustine's assertions: "What we call bad things are good things perverted."[7] When an accident blinds an eye, leaving a person sightless, we know it's bad; the loss of what's good, sight, makes it bad. Moral evil, like blindness—like the vacuum at the heart of a killer tornado—has power resulting from goodness lost. Thus the primal sin "arises when a conscious creature becomes more interested in itself than in God . . . and wishes to exist 'on its own.' . . . This is the sin of Pride."[8]

Consistently, in both fiction and nonfiction, Lewis insisted that pride, the spiritual sin that parades itself as a self-designed and self-actualized self, underlies all other forms of sin. As John

Milton envisioned, "The first creature who ever committed it was Satan 'the proud angel who turned from God to himself, not wishing to be subject, but to rejoice like a tyrant in having subjects of his own.'"[9] Thus we find in *Paradise Lost* a fallen angel whose "prime concern is with his own dignity," who pretends "that he exists 'on his own' in the sense of not having been created by God, 'self-begot, self-raised by his own quickening power.'"[10]

Like vandals defacing a Gothic cathedral, our sins senselessly ravage all that's good.

Evil acts, like pus flowing from pride's abscess—sins, trespasses, betrayals—are forms of sacrilege. We take something that's as good as sexual desire and demean it with lust and sodomy and pornography. To illustrate, Lewis noted that crowds of men collect to watch striptease acts. "Now suppose you came to a country where you could fill a theatre by simply bringing a covered plate on to the stage and then slowly lifting the cover so as to let every one see, just before the lights went out, that it contained a mutton chop or a bit of bacon, would you not think that in that country something had gone wrong with the appetite for food?"[11] Wholesome appetites, when disordered, breed disease. We take what's as pure as life-giving blood and soil it with heroin. We take the air our lungs crave and darken it with cigarette tar. As Lewis wrote, the "heinousness of sin" derives from the fact "that every sin is the distortion of an energy breathed into us—an energy which, if not thus distorted, would have blossomed into one of those holy acts whereof 'God did it' and 'I did it' are both true descriptions. We poison the wine as He decants it into us; murder a melody He would play with us as the instrument. We caricature the self-portrait He would paint. Hence all sin, whatever else it is, is sacrilege."[12]

Like vandals defacing a Gothic cathedral, our sins senselessly ravage all that's good, all that God's made. In its twisted self-serving, sin smears creation with its slime. Thus sin's ultimately far worse than childish errors or inadvertent moral lapses—it's an affront to God, a prideful rejection of His standards, His truth, His beauty—of all that stands rooted in His very being. Sin redefines reality just as gracelessly as "graffiti artists" foul public parks. It rewrites life's rules as poorly as screenwriters "update" Shakespeare's dramas.

Still more, sin is like a leech or an intestinal worm. It is parasitical. Here Augustine and Thomas Aquinas buttress the position Lewis took when he insisted sin is the privation of good. Sin has voracious power, but it's the power of a vacuum sucking things into its emptiness. It has no being of its own but drains away the life of its host. Like progressive blindness, sin robs the eye of its power to see, ravages its integrity. Sin, like internal bleeding, depletes a creature's substance, leeching away its life-giving blood. As Lewis said, goodness "is, so to speak, itself: badness is only spoiled goodness. And there must be something good first before it can be spoiled."[13]

So sin corrupts all it touches. Like AIDS it attacks our spiritual immune system. Designed to be holy, we deny our design and fail to be pure, losing our health. As Thomas Aquinas taught, sin shackles our souls, drags them down with chains, and forces them to stagger under the weight of four wounds: weakness; ignorance; malice; concupiscence (the lust of the flesh). Wanting what we want, seeking what pleases us, we sin and add to the contagion of evil corrupting the world.

Our sin, our deadly guerrilla war with God, misshapes us. For what we think about God makes us. Whatever gets our attention, as when some brokers lose track of all else in their fixation on stocks and bonds, gets us. Whatever we admire we acquire, as is evident when adolescents ape the swagger and style of adored musicians. Conversely, nothing more surely shrivels us than the emptiness of godless thoughts or the coldness of blood-less disloyalties! When we turn from the truth, what essentially is, and follow fantasies, the vanishing vapors of self-centeredness, we cut our life-giving roots and slowly wither away.

As Iris Murdoch, a British novelist, wrote: "The chief enemy of excellence in morality (and also in art) is personal fantasy: the tissue of self-aggrandizing and consoling wishes and dreams which prevents one from seeing what is there outside one."[14] We too easily believe lies, become addicted to lies, and crash through the guardrails of life's journey by following false signposts, taking fraudulent detours, using flawed maps.

In John's second letter, we're warned to beware of "antichrists"—deceivers who would derail us from the right rails of truth—"For many deceivers are entered into the world, who confess not that Jesus Christ is come in the flesh. This is a deceiver and an antichrist" (v. 7, KJV). In his first letter, John stressed that "even now are there many antichrists" (2:18, KJV), liars who deny "that Jesus is the Christ," who deny "the Father and the Son" (v. 22, KJV).

⌐ *"All sin is a kind of lying."* ⌐

In the Greek language, the prefix *anti-* means either opposition to or substitution for. Antichrists, thus, are those who oppose or set up rivals to Christ. John, the only biblical writer to use this word, used it here not to sketch a vision of a satanic figure at the end of time but as a description of those persons who deviously, deceitfully lure men away from God. Augustine said: "All sin is a kind of lying." What often seems (to all too many of us) a minor fault, in fact proves to be the most damning of sins, the underlying sin of sins, the dominant trait of all antichrists. As Lewis said: "Mr. [Charles] Williams has reminded us in unforgettable words that 'Hell is inaccurate', and has drawn attention to the fact that Satan lies about every subject he mentions in Paradise Lost."[15]

Sin's deceit gains graphic illustration in Lewis's *The Last Battle,* the capstone volume of the Narnian stories. It tells of the final struggle between the forces of good and evil. The mastermind of the evil forces was "the Ape" who managed to persuade many Narnians that Aslan and "Tash," the "terrible god" of the Calormenes "who fed on the blood of his people," were identical. Like many folks today, he declared "God" can be whatever we wish him to be! Like medieval "nominalists," influential teachers like the "Ape" claim our words link us to no objective reality, so they mean whatever we wish them to mean. However, Prince Rilian proclaimed the truth: "Ape," he cried with a great voice, "you lie. You lie damnably. You lie like a Calormene. You lie like an Ape."[16]

Yet the ape successfully deceived the masses. He found an old lion skin and forced a simpleminded donkey, Puzzle, to wear it. Ape's "devilish cunning" worked: "By mixing a little truth with it they had made their lie far stronger."[17] Only a faithful few saw through the lie and joined Aslan when the "last battle" ensued. The majority of the beasts and dwarfs joined the wrong side and, corrupted by the lies, followed the Ape to destruction. They won a local battle but lost their souls.

On a large scale, in instances at a distance from us, we easily discern and decry the lie. Hitler's propaganda attracts few advocates these days, though millions once embraced it. Snake oil advertisements in old magazines prod us to smile at earlier generations' gullibility, though we're equally vulnerable to slickly designed TV ads promising miracle cures. Millions of overweight Americans know they need diet and exercise, but they buy the lie that magic ointments and 10-day workouts will make them suddenly slim. We grandly grant the importance of telling the truth when we pillory Washington politicians caught in a web of deceit. Yet in our own little world we may weave similar fabrics of untruth. "False advertising" and "breech of contract" regularly lead to financial settlements in this nation's courts, yet we easily justify our own exaggerated claims and broken vows. In all this we are what N. Scott Peck called "people of the lie" and believers of lies. We so crave pleasure, or esteem, or profit, or position, that we easily believe a lie.

Yet, even though we may string together beads of deceit in office affairs, we don't want others to lie to us. Few things cause us greater pain or destroy our relationships more quickly than a lie unearthed, a betrayal brought to light. You don't want your spouse to lie to you even if you routinely lie to her! But Satan, the "father of lies," and the lying antichrists around us, lure us into unreality and illusion and error. These antichrists deceive us, make us think we're OK, tempt us to destroy ourselves by sailing about on the gusts of vapors. Thus evil pervades our world.

Humankind's original design has been blemished, warped, twisted into a pale likeness of God's will. The call to holiness must be preceded by a call to repent of, to be cleansed of, the sin that prevents it, "for all have sinned, and come short of the glory of God" (Rom. 3:23, KJV). In truth, "by one man sin entered into the world, and death by sin" (5:12, KJV). So with David we confess: "I acknowledge my transgressions: and my sin is ever before me" (Ps. 51:3, KJV). So "If we say that we have no sin, we deceive ourselves, and the truth is not in us" (1 John 1:8, KJV).

7 There's a Devil in This Mess

"The Bent One"

"I expect most witches are like that. They are not interested in things or people unless they can use them; they are terribly practical."[1]

"You're just like the Witch," said Polly. "All you think of is killing things."[2]

C. S. LEWIS FIRST REACHED A LARGE POPULAR AUDIENCE (as was evident in a *Time* magazine cover story devoted to him) with the publication of *The Screwtape Letters* in the 1940s. The book contains an imaginative series of letters from Screwtape, a high-ranking devil in hell, to Wormwood, his nephew, who is assigned to earth. The letters outline techniques to draw downward and ultimately damn a young man in England during World War II. The two tempters finally fail, however, when their target inadvertently slips out of their hands, killed by a Nazi bombing raid on London.

> ## Beyond belief, God intends to transform us. Satan schemes to entrap us.

Underlying the series of letters is a profound message: Satan and his ilk seek to subtly subvert a believer's salvation chiefly by preventing his growth in grace, his sanctification. Beyond be-

lief, God intends to transform us. So Satan, Lewis said elsewhere, schemes to entrap us: "Like a good chess player he is always trying to maneuver you into a position where you can
save your castle only by losing your bishop."[3]

Screwtape's letters make it clear that Lewis believed not only
in the pervasiveness of evil but in a very personal locus of evil—
Satan and his fallen followers. In a preface to a later edition of
the book, Lewis responded to a question concerning his belief
in devils, saying: "I do. That is to say, I believe in angels, and I
believe that some of these, by the abuse of their free will, have
become enemies of God and, as a corollary, to us. These we
may call devils. They do not differ in nature from good angels,
but their nature is depraved."[4] Although they have great powers,
as created beings they never rival God, or the "Enemy Above"
as Screwtape calls Him.

In hell, these fallen angels continually jockey for position, as
if whipping and maneuvering horses in a race, intent above all
on winning. Competitive, might-makes-right, dog-eat-dog policies prevail in hell. Ultimately Lewis imagined that the "devils
can, in a spiritual sense, eat one another; and us. Even in human life we have seen the passion to dominate, almost to di-
gest, one's fellow; to make his whole intellectual and emotional
life merely an extension of one's own—to hate one's hatreds
and resent one's grievances and indulge one's egoism through
him as well as through oneself."[5]

The same issue is addressed in one of Lewis's Narnian stories, *The Magician's Nephew*. This work contains a probing presentation of personified evil, a man who seems totally possessed by demonic powers, intent on controlling all within
reach. Andrew Ketterley, an elderly "magician" who dabbled in
the occult and sought (like Dr. Faustus) to use his knowledge to
transform nature, tricked and used his nephew Digory as an ex-
periment. Digory, however, with the cunning eye of a child,
shrewdly noted, "he thinks he can do anything he likes to get
anything he wants."[6]

Uncle Andrew himself, illustrating how one can be thoroughly transformed by Nietzsche's "transvaluation of all values," explains why he had remorselessly broken a promise to Digory's
mother, an act Digory labeled "rotten": "'Rotten?' said Uncle

Andrew with a puzzled look. 'Oh, I see. You mean that little boys ought to keep their promises. Very true: most right and proper, I'm sure, and I'm very glad you have been taught to do it. But of course you must understand that rules of that sort, however excellent they may be for little boys—and servants—and women—and even people in general, can't possibly be expected to apply to profound students and great thinkers and sages.'"[7] Much like Raskolnikov in Dostoyevsky's *Crime and Punishment,* Uncle Andrew styles himself autonomous, a law unto himself. As he explained to his nephew: "Men like me who possess hidden wisdom, are freed from common rules just as we are cut off from common pleasures. Ours, my boy, is a high and lonely destiny."[8] This attitude, making oneself a law unto himself, characterizes the proud persons who reject God.

When Digory and others, through Uncle Andrew's magic, are transported into another world, they there encounter a higher—or deeper and baser—source of evil. Here Lewis reintroduces a commanding figure earlier encountered by readers of the Narnian stories in *The Lion, the Witch, and the Wardrobe:* the White Witch, Queen Jadis, who had used her "Deplorable Word" to exterminate all that lived in Charn. Explaining her bloody actions in that realm, she said: "You must learn, child, that what would be wrong for you or any of the common people is not wrong in a great queen such as I. The weight of the world is on our shoulders. We must be freed from all rules. Ours is a high and lonely destiny."[9] At that point, "Digory suddenly remembered that Uncle Andrew had used exactly the same words."[10] Such Nietzschean will-to-power, the drive to dominate others, typifies the forces of hell.

> *There's no holy laughter in the darkened corridors haunted by demons.*

This is equally evident in the witch Jadis's strategies in *The Lion, the Witch, and the Wardrobe.* As the story begins, the children enter a formerly beautiful Narnia, now held hostage by the

witch. She ruled to destroy, turning warm, flesh-and-blood creatures into ice sculptures. It was always winter under her reign.
After meeting the witch in her sleigh, shortly after entering Narnia, Lucy and the other children learn from kindly creatures
that the "woman" they'd earlier met was an evil creature.

> **"The White Witch?" said Edmund, "who's she?"**
>
> **"She is a perfectly terrible person," said Lucy.**
>
> **"She calls herself the Queen of Narnia though she
> has no right to be queen at all, and all the Fauns and
> Dryads and Naiads and dwarfs and animals—at least all
> the good ones—simply hate her. And she can turn peo-
> ple into stone and do all kinds of horrible things. And
> she has made a magic so that it is always winter in Nar-
> nia—always winter, but it never gets to be Christmas."[11]**

There's an icy cold humorlessness in hell. If there are jokes,
they're malicious jibes and cynical slurs designed to cut down
others. There's no holy laughter in the darkened corridors haunted by demons. In his preface to *The Screwtape Letters,* Lewis
wrote: "'Satan,' said Chesterton, 'fell through force of gravity.' We
must picture Hell as a state where everyone is perpetually concerned about his own dignity and advancement, where everyone has a grievance, and where everyone lives the deadly seri-
ous passions of envy, self-importance, and resentment."[12] It's a
world much like the America of the 1990s—a complaint-ob-
sessed "nation of victims" that bewails imagined insults, airs
every hidden hint of anguish, and launches endless lawsuits.

Evil is, like sickness, ultimately the deprivation or absence of good.

The "reality" of all this evil is, Lewis teaches, rooted in the
reality of Satan. Though evil is, like sickness, ultimately the dep-
rivation or absence of good, it exerts much power in that it de-
praves existent beings, angels and humans. Its power is illustrated in Frank E. Peretti's popular novels, *This Present Darkness*
and its sequel, *Piercing the Darkness.* The title of the first book
comes from Eph. 6:12: "For we are not contending against flesh

and blood, but against the principalities, against the powers, against the world rulers of this present darkness" (RSV). That of the second comes from John 1:5: "The light shines in the darkness, and the darkness has not overcome it" (RSV). Peretti's central theme is spiritual warfare, an enduring conflict between demonic and angelic beings that becomes localized in human beings and activities.

Peretti takes seriously the reality of spiritual warfare, clearly a biblical teaching—and, incidentally, one central to the monastic movement of the Early Church, where monks like Anthony went to the desert to do battle with the forces of evil. Always, the Christian tradition insists, we do battle with demonic beings that are over against us, not indwelling us. One of the great spiritual masters, Francisco de Osuna, insists, in *The Third Spiritual Alphabet,* that "if you wish to be spiritual you must regard yourself as a spiritual warrior."[13] He understands that the demonic powers attack us from without. Yet we must always remember that, "as Saint Bernard says, our enemy is weak and can vanquish only the people who wish defeat."[14]

Whether or not we're aware of it, we're engaged in spiritual warfare. "The war against evil spirits," says philosopher Peter Kreeft, "is no less real and terrible than the war against any flesh and blood enemy. The greatest war in history was not World War II but this spiritual war, and we're in it now."[15] Moral relativists and moral traditionalists cannot coexist! Secular humanists and sacramental theists cannot share the same pulpit. Those who insist there are no truths cannot but conflict with those who believe in divine truths. Those who contend there is no sin cannot but dislike those who staunchly remind them of its slime.

This spiritual conflict is markedly evident in another of the Narnian stories, *The Silver Chair,* which chronicles the adventures of some children the lion Aslan dispatched to rescue Prince Rilian. In time they enter the realm of "the Lady of the Green Kirtle," the witch who had bewitched Rilian. She tries her best to persuade the children, and a fascinating creature—a "Marsh-wiggle"—named Puddleglum—that "Narnia" itself as well as Aslan were illusions. They struggle to retain memories of the truth, Aslan's principal concern, tempted to consider only the here and now. As skilled a propagandist as Hitler, orchestrating mass torch-lit meetings, the witch leads the children in chants, designed to dull the mind by repetition:

> **"There never was such a world," said the Witch.**
>
> **"No," said Jill and Scrubb, "never was such a world."**
>
> **"There never was any world but mine," said the Witch.**
>
> **"There never was any world but yours," said they.**[16]

Alone among the little troop, the Marsh-wiggle resisted the witch's blandishments. Her world was not the real world! So, he said: "But you can play that fiddle till your fingers drop off, and still you won't make me forget Narnia; and the whole Overworld too. You may have blotted it out and turned it dark like this, for all I know. Nothing more likely. But I know I was there once. I've seen the sky full of stars. I've seen the sun coming up out of the sea of a morning and sinking behind the mountains at night. And I've seen him up in the midday sky when I couldn't look at him for brightness."[17]

His speech awakened the others! They suddenly saw the truth:

> **"Why, there it is!" cried the Prince. "Of course! The blessing of Aslan upon this honest Marsh-wiggle. We have all been dreaming, these last few minutes. How could we have forgotten it? Of course we've all seen the sun."**
>
> **"By Jove, so we have!" said Scrubb. "Good for you Puddleglum! You're the only one of us with any sense, I do believe."**[18]

The struggle continues, a battle of wills between the witch and her captives, until finally the children escape, freed at last by faint memories of the truth that overcame the lies of the witch.

In Lewis's space trilogy, we find other examples of demonic possession in persons such as Weston, the scientist who wants to "spread spirituality" on the new planet of Perelandra, then to dominate the cosmos for the "good" of a "Force" that impelled him. Meeting him in the early pages of *Perelandra,* Ransom was overwhelmed by the sensation that "this, in fact was not a man," for the old Weston had disappeared and the "Un-man" had taken up residence.

Facing his old antagonist from *Out of the Silent Planet,* Ransom saw the "Un-man" smile "a devilish smile," and he "realized that he had never taken the words seriously." The smile "did not defy goodness, it ignored it to the point of annihilation."[19] The demonic Weston had become the very antithesis of God's design in creating man. "Weston's body, traveling in a space-ship, had been the bridge by which something else had invaded Perelandra—whether that supreme and original evil whom in Mars they call The Bent One, or one of his lesser followers, made no difference."[20]

On Perelandra, Ransom, representing the forces of righteousness, ultimately defeated and destroyed, through hand-to-hand combat, the Un-man. On earth, however, Adam and Eve had earlier caved in and lost their Lord's estate. Consequently, planet Earth is "enemy-occupied territory—that is what this world is. Christianity is the story of how the rightful king has landed, you might say landed in disguise, and is calling us all to take part in a great campaign of sabotage."[21] Our struggle with sin has cosmic roots, for sin's source is Satan, the "bent one" in hell.

Lewis's vision clearly derives from the prophet Isaiah, who cried: "How art thou fallen from heaven, O Lucifer, son of the morning! how art thou cut down to the ground, which didst weaken the nations! For thou hast said in thine heart, I will ascend into heaven, I will exalt my throne above the stars of God: I will sit also upon the mount of the congregation, in the sides of the north: I will ascend above the heights of the clouds; I will be like the most High. Yet thou shalt be brought down to hell, to the sides of the pit" (Isa. 14:12-15, KJV).

8   We Choose to Lose Our Way

"The Fall Is Simply Disobedience"

"The one principle of hell is—'I am my own.'"[1]

"Evil comes from the abuse of free will."[2]

*W*ERE IT NOT FOR SIN WE'D BE HOLY AS DESIGNED, following the Creator's guidelines for the right way, enjoying a healthy life. But we've lost our original goodness, strayed afar from our proper end. We've crushed our moral compass, slipped away from our true design, forgotten our primordial blueprint. So an accurate understanding of sin precedes any clear call to holy living. All we know of salvation presumes an accurate understanding of sin.

Certain skewed definitions of sin trivialize it, reducing it to genial shortcomings or ignorant mistakes, suggesting we can eliminate its influence with the use of self-help manuals or self-esteem exercises. Other flawed definitions exaggerate sin, suggesting it's so powerful and formative that we're condemned, like plantation slaves, to submit to its control. As long as we live, some say, sin reigns, sitting supremely on dictator's throne, making any sin-free thoughts or actions impossible and canceling any form of Christian holiness.

Consequently, those who urge Christians to actually seek to "be holy" generally share John Wesley's conviction that "nothing is sin, strictly speaking, but a voluntary transgression of a known law of God. Therefore, every voluntary breach of the law of love is sin; and nothing else, if we speak properly."[3] Though C. S. Lewis never (to my knowledge) cited Wesley as a theological authority, he shared Wesley's affirmation of "free will." Thus his definition of "sin" parallels Wesley's. Lewis wrote: "Man is now a horror to God and to himself and a creature ill-adapted to the universe not because God made him so but because he has made himself so by the abuse of his free will."[4] Both Wesley and Lewis took seriously the godly power of free will and the demonic consequences of its misuse through sin in human history.

In significant ways man's fall, as deeply as any single theme, shapes Lewis's works. It alone underlies and explains the unexplainable follies and brutalities that mark human history. Musing on Milton's portrayal of the Fall in *Paradise Lost*, Lewis noted that Eve, barely created, "sees herself in a pool of water, and falls in love with her own reflection. Then God makes her look up, and she sees Adam. But the interesting point is that the first sight of Adam is a disappointment; he is a much less immediately attractive object than herself."[5]

Like the mythical Narcissus, gazing at his reflection in a pool, we fall in love with ourselves.

Like the mythical Narcissus, gazing at his reflection in a pool, we fall in love with ourselves; we find nothing other than ourselves worth noting. We even reduce all "truth" to what inwardly pleases us. We take as our motto the title of Luigi Pirandello's play: *Right You Are If You Think You Are!* Some even imagine they can freely "define reality" and then create computerized castles in cybernetic worlds they choose to inhabit! Nothing, not even God, matters as much as oneself!

In his outer space romances, Lewis contrasts the unfallen worlds of Malacandra (Mars) and Perelandra (Venus) with the sin-bent, darkened world of Thulcandra (Earth). The Narnian stories frequently emphasize the difference between fallen and pristine creatures. When, in *Prince Caspian,* Lucy inquired about "the old Narnians," who had earlier lived in the land, she was told: "'Why, that's us,' said the Dwarf. 'We're a kind of rebellion, I suppose.'"[6]

Thus sin results not from weakness but from disobedience. Specific sins may well result from weakness, but it's *sin,* the inner spirit of rebellion that constitutes sin. Like the nervous system that moves the muscles to act, sin prods us to do evil acts. To Lewis, the Early Church fathers' understanding of Adam's fall helps explain the human predicament. As he says: "The Fathers may sometimes say that we are punished for Adam's sin: but they much more often say that we sinned 'in Adam.' It may be impossible to find out what they meant by this, or we may decide that what they meant was erroneous. But I do not think we can dismiss their way of talking as a mere 'idiom.' Wisely, or foolishly, they believed that we were really—and not simply by legal fiction—involved in Adam's action."[7]

Both Scripture and human experience amply illustrate both the sin (singular) and sins (plural) that, like paint dribbled from leaky buckets, stud the stories of our race. One sins because of what Lewis called the deeper bent toward evil—sin singular—which Paul said "dwelleth in me" (Rom. 7:17, KJV). The plaguelike persistence of original sin, the indelible ink of our bent-toward-evil, stains every page of human history. In his discussion of Milton's *Paradise Lost,* Lewis wrote: "The Fall is simply and solely Disobedience—doing what you have been told not to do: and it results from Pride—from being too big for your boots, forgetting your place, thinking that you are God."[8] He explains: "The classic biblical text Milton develops shows that: Eve's arguments in favour of eating the Apple are, in themselves, reasonable enough; the answer to them consists simply in the reminder 'You mustn't. You were told not to.' 'The great moral which reigns in Milton,' said Addison, 'is the most universal and most useful that can be imagined, that Obedience to the will of God makes men happy and that Disobedience makes them miserable.'"[9]

When we disobey we refuse to trust God, to take Him at His Word. Disbelief prompts us to turn our backs on God. We trot out our own plans and plot out our own agendas, refusing to accept the fact that God created us according to His plan and has His own agenda. Defying Him, we fail to love Him. Like pouting children refusing to eat green peas, even though ice cream is promised for dessert, we refuse to do His will—which is that we return to Him and share His love.

Unable to love, our souls go aground like rudderless ships and capsize in the seas of fear and anxiety. "Bent creatures are full of fears," said Elwin Ransom, standing transfixed in the presence of Oyarsa, the angelic ruler of Malacandra in *Out of the Silent Planet*.[10] Our fears, like box office film attractions, feature overwhelming catastrophes and improbable, oft-imaginary losses. Thus, in *The Screwtape Letters* Screwtape tells his nephew to never forget, while tempting his earthly target, that God—"The Enemy"—"wants men to be concerned with what they do; our business is to keep them thinking about what will happen to them."[11]

> ## *This desire to stay in control, to master our own destiny, ultimately damns us.*

Fearing failure, misfortune, or death, we frantically grope about, clasping at autumn leaves adrift in the wind, clinging to astrological forecasts or stock market schemes rather than resting comfortably in the arms of our loving Heavenly Father. Yet in the end, as we discover in Lewis's first "Christian" treatise, *The Pilgrim's Regress,* "security is mortals' greatest enemy."[12] Thus much sin stems from our frantic efforts to secure our place, to build walls around our castles, where we can keep control of ourselves, our possessions, our families, whatever we can brand "ours."

This desire to stay in control, to master our own destiny, ultimately damns us. Indeed, Screwtape said, getting a man to forget "the eternal and the Present"—especially to "live in the Future"—eases him from God's reality into Satan's unreality. "In a word, the Future is, of all things, the thing least like eternity. It is the most completely temporal part of time—for the Past is frozen and no longer flows, and the Present is all lit up with eternal rays."[13]

Various utopian schemes have enlisted converts who have promoted such fantasies as Jacobism in France, which, in the 1790s, set heads rolling from the Guillotine, or Marxist Communism, which led to the deaths of multiplied millions around the world in the 20th century. Closer to home, the same utopianism courses through much of Lyndon B. Johnson's "Great Society," with its "war on poverty" and blithe promises of a Washington-ruled land free of pain, inequality, and uncertainty. All these utopian schemes stress future perfection. As one French utopian socialist insisted: "Nothing is impossible for a government that wants the good of its citizens."[14] The utopian mind-set is graphically evident in *The Lost Landscape,* by William H. Whyte Jr., a study of urban planning. The planners generally include everything imaginable—shopping centers, recreation facilities, educational and artistic institutions. Only one thing is never part of the plan: a cemetery! A perfect world cannot tolerate the reality of death!

The story of the ancient Tower of Babel replays like an endless echo down the canyons of history. Forever we find prophets (secular humanists in our day) promising heavens-on-earth if we just follow their formulae. And almost always their visions collapse into nightmares when enacted. In Lewis's judgment: "Hence nearly all vices are rooted in the Future. Gratitude looks to the Past and love to the Present; fear, avarice, lust, and ambition look ahead."[15] Accordingly, Jesus said, "Take therefore no thought for the morrow: for the morrow shall take thought for the things of itself. Sufficient unto the day is the evil thereof" (Matt. 6:34, KJV).

With imaginative insight, Lewis, in *Perelandra,* the second volume of his space trilogy, portrays this primal temptation as the desire to abandon the floating islands assigned to the Green Lady, to disobey instructions and move to the "Fixed Land," thereby becoming less dependent on God. Ultimately, after Ransom had defeated and killed the evil genius Weston, thus saving Perelandra from demonic attack, the Green Lady (the "Queen" of the Perelandra) said: "'As soon as you had taken away the Evil One,' she said, 'and I awoke from sleep, my mind was cleared. . . . The reason for not yet living on the Fixed Land is now so plain. How could I wish to live there except because it was Fixed? And why should I desire the Fixed except to make sure—to be able on one day to command where I should be the next and what should happen to me?'"[16]

She'd been tempted to trust herself rather than her Lord, to "draw my hands out of Maleldil's, to say to Him, 'Not thus, but thus'—to put in our own power what times should roll towards us"[17] and, like the ancient Israelites, hoard manna rather than trust Him to supply it. She discovered, however, resisting temptation, that "'that would have been cold love and feeble trust. And out of it how could we ever have climbed back into love and trust again?' 'I see it well,' said Ransom. 'Though in my world it would pass for folly. We have been evil so long. . . .'"[18]

Unlike the Green Lady, most of us grow dissatisfied with day-to-day dependence. Wanting to steer our own course, determined to build our secure households or cities or civilizations, we allow our anxieties to prod us into distrust, the converse of faith. Unable to cope with uncertainty, finding it difficult to trust God with our future, rejecting Jesus' admonition to "not be anxious," losing the courage to relax and just be creatures, we flounder in "unfaith."

In sum, Lewis wrote: "I willingly believe that the damned are, in one sense, successful, rebels to the end; that the doors of hell are locked on the inside. I do not mean that their ghosts may not wish to come out of hell, in the vague fashion wherein an envious man 'wishes' to be happy: but they certainly do not will even the first preliminary stages of that self-abandonment through which alone the soul can reach any good."[19]

What's lost in hell is what John urged in his first letter: "And hereby we do know that we know him, if we keep his commandments. He that saith, I know him, and keepeth not his commandments, is a liar, and the truth is not in him. But whoso keepeth his word, in him verily is the love of God perfected: hereby know we that we are in him. He that saith he abideth in him ought himself also so to walk, even as he walked" (1 John 2:3-6, KJV).

9 ✍ The Ravages of Sin

"The Soul Has Gone Out of the Wood"

"The soul has gone out of the wood and water.
Oh, I daresay you could awake them; a little.
But it would not be enough. A storm, or even a
river-flood would be of little avail against our
present enemy. Your weapon would break in
your hands. For the Hideous Strength confronts
us and it is as in the days when Nimrod
built a tower to reach heaven." . . .
"No power that is merely earthly," he continued
at last, "will serve against the Hideous Strength."
"Then let us all to prayers," said Merlinus.[1]

WHEN ILLNESS NUDGES US TO THE DOCTOR'S OFFICE, we seek an accurate diagnosis of our plight as much as relief from our pain. Uncertainty with what's wrong often disturbs us more than the disease itself. Indeed, I've sometimes been delivered from worrisome symptoms of disease simply by having them rightly diagnosed! Before swallowing pills or submitting to surgery, we want to know why we're ill, to understand why prescribed drugs or techniques might work. To a degree, we just want to know, to dissolve the unknowns of disease with the solvent of truth. We also want, if we're wise, to alter toxic behaviors that may have caused, or now add to, our sufferings.

C. S. Lewis, especially in fictional works such as *That Hideous Strength,* envisioned the lethal power of sin that, like a deadly plague, corrupts individuals, societies, and even planet earth itself. Adam's fall infects and paralyzes societies as well as individuals. To Lewis, the modern world, a world that has lost its soul, clearly illustrates sin's corrosive power.

Meredith Veldman, *in Fantasy, the Bomb, and the Greening of Britain: Romantic Protest, 1945-1980,*[2] includes C. S. Lewis in his study of the "romantic protest" currents that swirled together in their antipathy to certain aspects of "modernity." In his judgment, the "fantasy" literature of J. R. R. Tolkien and Lewis, as well as the "small-is-beautiful" environmentalists influenced by E. F. Schumacher, shared a nostalgic distaste for 20th-century technological society.

Veldman defines "romanticism" as "the belief that the empirical and analytical methods of modern science cannot comprehend all of reality, that truth in its wholeness extends beyond the reach of the physical senses."[3] Firmly rooted in this fertile "romantic" soil, two of the Oxford "Inklings," Lewis and Tolkien, drafted fantasies that struck a responsive chord in readers, ultimately becoming "two of the most popular writers in twentieth-century Britain."[4] Both clearly disliked much about the modern world, holding that much of value in earlier times had been destroyed.

Their love for other worlds, better worlds, obviously helped shape their fiction. Lewis's space trilogy and *The Chronicles of Narnia* and Tolkien's *The Lord of the Rings* celebrated the virtues of earlier eras. For both authors, such imaginative works were "religious" acts, bearing witness to spiritual realities smothered by the smoke of technological "progress." Both sought to craft stories that would bring readers back to the fundamental truths necessary for the truly good life.

In Lewis's novel, *That Hideous Strength,* one of the demonic architects of the National Institute of Co-ordinated Experiments, Lord Feverstone, recruited a young sociologist, Mark. To explain the scientific objectives of the institute, he declared: "Man has got to take charge of Man."[5] This, of course, meant an elite, powerful oligarchy would seize control of society. Asked what policies it would institute, Feverstone proposed: "Quite simple and obvious things, at first—sterilization of the unfit, liquidation of backward races (we don't want any dead weights), selective breeding. Then real education, including pre-natal education."[6] To Mark's astonished response, "This is stupendous," Feverstone agreed, declaring: "It's the real thing at last. A new type of man: and it's people like you who've got to begin to make him."[7]

> *Much that troubles our world,*
> *Lewis believed, derives from*
> *our failure to grasp*
> *the nature of nature,*
> *the truth of creation.*

Such "new men" would finally rule a barren planet, for another N.I.C.E. insider declared that the planet would be shorn—much as Delilah shaved Samson's locks—of all vegetation. "It sounds," said Mark, "like abolishing pretty well all organic life." Assenting, the man said: "And why not? It is simple hygiene." As he reasoned, "In us organic life has produced Mind. It has done its work. After that we want no more of it. We do not want the world any longer furred over with organic life, like what you call the blue mould—all sprouting and budding and breeding and decaying. We must get rid of it."[8]

Such utopian visions forever seek to undo creation in order to redo it to our standards. Much that troubles our world, Lewis believed, derives from this desire, from our failure to grasp the nature of nature, the truth of creation. Consequently, mistaken ideas give birth to misguided actions. Issues as diverse as AIDS and abortion stem from modern man's failure to grasp and abide by the nature of nature, his refusal to accept truth about reality.

To a Christian like Lewis, Mother Nature aches and wastes away like a cancer victim because we abuse her. Despite our marvelous ability to think, we fail to think prudently, we really fail to see things as they are. We've lost that "metaphysical realism" that undergirded solid classical cultures. A contemporary American philosopher, Hilary Putnam, admits: "It is impossible to find a philosopher before Kant (and after the pre-Socratics) who was not a metaphysical realist."[9]

To recover it, one of America's most prestigious philosophers, William P. Alston, recently published *A Realist Conception of Truth,* persuasively arguing that realism is the best philosophical stance for those concerned with truth.[10] Alston declares that the way we "think about truth" determines much that we do. Alston's approach, like Lewis's, is rooted in 2,000 years of Western philosophy, wherein thinkers such as Aristotle have insisted that "truth" rightly aligns us with what is "real." We live in an objectively real world, a world other than us. When we discern "truth" we conform our minds, like plaster in a mold, to what is. Thus we formulate "truth" in propositions. I say things such as "Washington, D.C., is the capital of the United States" and "there are mountains in Colorado." Virtually all the statements I make, virtually all the thoughts I have, take such declarative form, and they presume the objective reality of a world independent of my mind.

The opposite view, often espoused as forms of "idealism," contends that our minds fabricate a world, that it is as we *think* or *will* it to be. We hear much about such views in "postmodern" publications, where we're endlessly informed about "social constructions" or "personal interpretations" of reality. "Reality is whatever you want it to be," today's gurus declare. Such approaches inevitably make the world mind-dependent rather than the mind world-dependent. Allegedly different conceptual schemes render radically different portraits of the world, and all "truth" is found within us, not outside us.

> *When we fail to understand
> creation according to
> the Creator's plan,
> we easily turn to fouling it up!*

To illustrate: when, as a realist, I say "the sun is shining," I refer not to my hopes or fantasies but to the fact that a very real sun's rays are striking the very solid earth around me! The sun's light is a given. I see the sun because it's really there, presenting itself to my mind. Were there no sun, I'd never have imagined one. In fact, I can imagine nothing that is not some representation or distortion of real things. Remembering and thinking about the sun is not the same as seeing it, but without the initial seeing there would be no thinking or remembering.

Though not demanding it, Alston's realism perfectly suits theism. Indeed, he concludes: truth is finally determined "by the way things are," though "this 'subjection' to stubborn, unyielding facts beyond" us "seems powerfully repugnant, even intolerable to many."[11] As a Christian, Alston, sees this as "a special case of the original sin, insisting on human autonomy and control and refusing to be subservient to that on which our being and our fate depends, which for the Christian is God."[12] Theists like Alston and Lewis take seriously God's Lordship, His transcendence. He is Real, He is Ultimate Being, and as Creator He stands above us! So, too, He created beings, specific entities, independent of us. When we fail to understand creation according to the Creator's plan, we easily turn to fouling it up! We fail to think truthfully and to live wisely.

The essence of this failure was glimpsed with prophetic power early in the 17th century by John Donne, one of Lewis's favorite poets. He feared the emergent "new philosophy," constipated with rationalism and doubt, was so nearsighted that:

> The sun is lost, and the earth, and no man's wit
> Can well direct him where to look for it.
> And freely men confess that this world's spent,
>
> . . . .
>
> 'Tis all in pieces, all coherence gone.[13]

Donne feared that such narrow self-centeredness, such self-absorbed humanism, drives a wedge between us and the rest of creation. It's an adolescent affliction that renders one peculiarly oblivious to one's surroundings and condescending, even contemptuous of one's home. Donne's fears seem confirmed in the more recent lines of W. B. Yeats's "The Second Coming":

> Turning and turning in the widening gyre
> The falcon cannot hear the falconer;
> Things fall apart; the centre cannot hold;
> Mere anarchy is loosed upon the world.[14]

Things fall apart, in part, because of our ignorance. For all our cognitive powers, we routinely stumble into pits—veritable cosmic dark holes—of ignorance. For all our scientific information, we lack the wisdom to live well. Nutritionally misguided, we easily err believing it's as good to eat fruitcake as fruit—or to substitute pie for bread! Too late too many of us learn valuable truths, truths necessary to live wisely and well.

This clearly applies to our behavior on planet earth. Lacking knowledge, we've blundered, like children trying to do intricate needlework, leaving jagged stitches, soiled patches, on the land's tapestry. We've too often failed to hear creation's music, to wonder at life's mysteries, to smell the just-plowed soil's freshness, to taste the ripe persimmon's sweetness, to see our small niche in an organically complex world. We've misweighed it, imagining it infinite; we've misjudged its texture, imagining the web of life's woven of stainless steel cables rather than silken threads. And when we fail to grasp the truth about creation, we inevitably fail to know truth about its Creator.

In part, our ignorance results from our educational system, especially where it's become an irreligious training program that makes no allowance for any transcendent reality, no place for traditional philosophy, no room for God in the cosmos. With unusual prescience, Lewis detected such trends in a series of lectures published as *The Abolition of Man*. As he noted, in the past wise teachers sought to "conform the soul to reality, and the solution had been knowledge, self-discipline, and virtue."[15] What's missing in modern education is precisely what guided earlier educators, who made moral distinctions between good and evil: "St. Augustine defines virtue as ordo amoris, the ordinate condition of the affections in which every object is accorded that kind and degree of love which is appropriate to it. Aristotle says that the aim of education is to make the pupil like and dislike what he ought. . . . Plato before him had said the same."[16] To Lewis, the consensus of the world's wisest teachers upheld "the doctrine of objective value, the belief that certain attitudes are really true, and others really false, to the kind of thing the universe is and the kind of things we are."[17]

The opposite approach is taken by "modern" educators who seek to conform reality to the human mind, to allege that we "construct" the world in accord with our desires! In many ways

Weston, a figure in the first two of Lewis's science fiction stories (*Out of the Silent Planet* and *Perelandra*) represents the "modern mind" that Lewis found not only objectionable but positively lethal. Back on earth after his first journey, to Malacandra (Mars), the central character, Ransom, warned: "And we have also evidence—increasing almost daily—that 'Weston,' or the force or forces behind 'Weston,' will play a very important part in the events of the next few centuries, and, unless we prevent them, a very disastrous one."[18]

> *Humanists live for the here and*
> *now, not any other and eternal—*
> *for the pleasurable moment,*
> *not eternal blessedness.*

Weston represented the mechanistic way of thinking that emerged some 500 years ago as currents of the Renaissance (A.D. 1300-1600) swirled into the stream of western civilization, muddying its current. Unlike medieval thinkers, who generally accepted the world as one well-designed by God, as an arena wherein one prepares for eternity, modern technicians have aggressively sought to improve their world so as to better enjoy things here and now. The natural world, earlier viewed as God's handiwork, has increasingly been treated as an assemblage of "natural resources" suitable for human engineering. "Progress," defined as the constant addition of acquisitions, whether personal or national, became more and more Westerners' driving concern. "Economics" increasingly replaced religion as their constant preoccupation. Ironically, the result, described in Lewis's first Christian treatise, *Pilgrim's Regress*, has backfired: "Their labour-saving devices multiply drudgery; their aphrodisiacs make them impotent; their amusements bore them; their rapid production of food leaves half of them starving, and their devices for saving time have banished leisure from their country."[19]

If "man is the measure," as moderns assert, our religion, our "ultimate concern," that which seeks to retie us with what's truly real and worthwhile, tends to center on us. David Ehrenfeld, in a probing study titled *The Arrogance of Humanism,* identifies its religious heart: absolute "faith" in reason and in our ability to manhandle our world to achieve unending social progress through scientific and technical means. Thus "committed to an unquestioning faith in the power of reason," humanism devalues any realities, be they supernatural or irrational, beyond human control. Humanists live for the here and now, not any other and eternal—for the pleasurable moment, not eternal blessedness.

Despite its professed "naturalism," however, humanism entails "a strong anti-Nature" bias, Ehrenfeld says, demeaning anything other than man. So, he indicates, "the principal humanist assumption" simply asserts: "All problems are soluble by people." Consequently, a cluster of correlates follow: infinite social improvement and technological development are possible; better replacements will be found for apparently limited natural resources such as petroleum; "human civilization will survive."[20]

With Ehrenfeld, Lewis thought that modern, scientific humanism clearly exposes our species' pride, that ancient hubris so condemned by ancient Greek and Christian thinkers. What slowly transpired, as modernity displaced the medieval world, was the elevation of pride to a positive virtue. Note the emphasis on "self-esteem" in all sectors of our society! In a grade school classroom, a banner declares: "We applaud ourselves," and in another class the children recite a marvelous mantra: "I am me and I am enough." Thus we find popular calls to "look out for number one," to abandon relationships that no longer "meet our needs," to do whatever "feels good," to consume natural resources however we please, to create social systems for our own good without concern for the debt heaped on our descendants, illustrating little if any concern for coming generations. For if humankind is the "measure" of all things, we alone matter and the physical world has value only when it serves our immediate purpose. Rather than being created by divine power, men and women create with a power that is divine.

PART FOUR

GOD'S HOLY PROVISIONS
"THE WHOLE OF CHRISTIANITY"

The Master Plan
for the Master's People

10 Called to Be Holy

"People of a Particular Sort"

*We might think that God wanted simply obedience
to a set of rules: whereas He really wants
people of a particular sort.*[1]

ON MARCH 16, 1778, ENERGIZED BY THE NEWLY FOUND FREEDOM of the American Revolution, the legislature of New York adopted a state motto, a Latin word to be placed on the state seal that visually portrayed a rising sun. The motto was *Excelsior!* Higher! The aspirations of the new nation, the embryonic United States of America, resided in that motto. There was a longing for the best, the finest form of government, the highest quality of life.

Ironically, the "democratic" society established by the American Revolution, and carbon copied throughout much of the world, has often diluted such aspirations. By encouraging equality democracies easily discourage quality. In *The Republic,* Plato likened a democracy to a ship whose sailors staged a mutiny and sought to steer the vessel on their own. Unfortunately, lacking expertise in navigation, their prospects of a safe voyage grow decidedly dim as the journey continues! So, too, in a society where every person insists "equality" to everyone else, any recognition of "excellence" tends to be disdained. Mediocrity rules! So, Lewis argued that equality

has no place in the world of the mind. Beauty is not democratic; she reveals herself more to the few than to the many, more to the persistent and disciplined seekers than to the careless. Virtue is not democratic;

she is achieved by those who pursue her more hotly
than most men. Truth is not democratic; she demands
special talents and special industry in those to whom
she gives her favours. Political democracy is doomed if
it tries to extend its demand for equality into these
higher spheres. Ethical, intellectual, or aesthetic democracy is death.[2]

The rejection of this position, as Lewis's underworld tempter, Screwtape, observed in his speech at the "Annual Dinner of
the Tempters' Training College for Young Devils," has led, during the past century, to a "vast overall movement towards the
discrediting, and finally the elimination of every kind of human
excellence—moral, cultural, social or intellectual."[3]

Yet we cannot forever escape this truth: excellence deserves
respect. When a gifted young athlete, Tiger Woods, won the
Masters Golf Tournament at the age of 21, setting a course
record at the same time, most of us applauded! When an aging
John Elway finally led the Denver Broncos to a SuperBowl victo-
ry, most of us admired his skill. And most of us, at least now
and then, admit to longing to attain similar goals. As youngsters
we envisioned playing professional baseball or starring on
Broadway. As adults we collaborate and compose "mission
statements" for churches or schools, filled with lofty goals. Admittedly, our proposals outstrip our abilities. Most of us have
learned, often in painful ways, the validity of Murphy's Law: "If
anything can go wrong, it will." (Adding a tag, someone said:
"Murphy was an optimist!")

> *We're often most aware of the*
> *grandeur of our actual potential*
> *when surrounded by the debris*
> *of our most flagrant failures.*

Such ironic "laws" reveal our fears about, as well as our experiences with, the "worsts" of life. We know how rarely things
are at their best. More importantly, they flash on the screen of

our consciences the truth that we are rarely at our best. Yet, interestingly enough, we're often most aware of the grandeur of our actual potential when surrounded by the debris of our most flagrant failures. Thus life's worsts often elicit humor, for we sense the gap between what is and what ought to be. We know that life should be lived at its best, that the bests should earmark our efforts. Yet how rarely the demonstrable bests stride across the stage of one's life!

When we add the suffix "est" to a word we lift it to a singular pinnacle. Only one can be an *est!* There's only one *est* to a category. Mount Everest, soaring more than 29,000 feet into the sky, is the world's *highest* mountain. The Amazon River, stretching 3,900 miles from the Andes to the Atlantic, is the world's *longest* river. The Pacific Ocean, encompassing 70,000,000 square miles, is earth's *largest* ocean. Some things are, absolutely, the *est* of all!

> ## There's something in each of us that wants to know what's best, that wants to become the best!

And there's something in each of us that wants to know what's best, that wants to become the best! We want our children's soccer teams to be the best in the league. We like to imagine the local high school is one of the "ten best" in the nation. We take pride in the "all-American" status of our city. Accordingly, Paul tells us, in 1 Cor. 12:31, that in life there's an ultimate, something that's truly best, the finest of the fine. It's the *summum bonum,* the highest good. So he follows the superlative modifier, "most," with the adjective "excellent" (or, as the Greek says, "beyond all comparison").

We admire what's truly excellent, for we're aware, as Plato declared: "Excellent things are rare." Yet they exist! However, rare, they are there. A business writer, Tom Peters, coauthored *In Search of Excellence* and *A Passion for Excellence,* books that indicate only a few American corporations deserve to be called "excellent." Those that deserve the label, Peters shows, all share a common commitment to high standards. A Mercedes-Benz advertisement summed up its operative rule, saying, "Excellence begins with how high you set your standards."

Excellence begins with how high you set your standards! All of us, in our best moments, long for the best, the finest attainable quality of life. Holiness sets high standards, urges spiritual excellence. In Jesus' words, excellence comes from responding to this challenge: "Be perfect," he said, "just as your Father in heaven is perfect" (Matt. 5:48, NKJV). All too often we ignore Jesus' command, taking comfort in "cheap grace" alternatives. Unfortunately, in many Christian circles, "grace" becomes a code word for "mediocrity" that is both touted and celebrated! Thus for many, the word *perfection,* like the word *holiness,* carries with it a strange stigma, an aura of impossibility.

Holiness is the way to be *fully human.*

Rather than take Jesus at His word, we accept our culture's soft bromide: "Nobody's perfect." Yet, to use biblical language, to be perfect is to be holy. So Peter insisted: "But just as he who called you is holy, so be holy in all you do; for it is written: 'Be holy, because I am holy'" (1 Pet. 1:15-16). We're called to be holy simply because we're designed to be holy. Mercedes-Benz automobiles are designed to run well—and they do. They're *excellent* cars! "Excellence begins with how high you set your standards." Similarly, we're designed to live well, to be persons of integrity. Holiness is our standard, the proper way to *be* fully human.

In *The Screwtape Letters,* the devil Screwtape urges his nephew-tempter Wormwood to keep his human subject ignorant of his true nature. If we're lost in a fog without a compass, we rarely blunder into the valley we're seeking. If we can be persuaded we're nothing but animals, we'll end up acting thusly. Blinded to the truth of our design, we're easily sucked into behaviors and beliefs truly beneath our dignity. For God "wants each man, in the long run, to be able to recognize all creatures (even himself) as glorious and excellent things."[4]

Christ's call to "perfection" means we're supposed to reach the goal for which God designed us. This has nothing to do with any utopian "perfection," nothing at all resembling the unattainable "classless state" of Marxist mythology, which ever eludes attainability. It's not becoming as physically attractive as film stars or as strong as professional athletes. Christian "perfection" is in fact quite down-to-earth and doable. The singular and eminently attainable goal for which we should strive, C. S. Lewis taught, is holiness: the sincere soul-surrender that unites us with God and the developing virtuous character that results from that union.

As mentioned in chapter 1, Lewis awakened to the possibility of holiness when, as a schoolboy, he read George MacDonald's *Phantases*. Though in his own mind a confirmed atheist, the book opened his heart (ever longing for "joy") to the possibility of higher realms of reality. It was "as if I had died in the old country and could never remember how I came alive in the new," and the "new" reality he encountered was "the bright shadow" of "holiness."[5]

> ## The "bright shadow" of holiness subsequently drew him God-ward.

This is a crucial passage for understanding the aura of holiness streaming through the works of Lewis. He had, in the deepest part of his heart, discovered a holy realm, a divine dimension for which his heart hungered, and he never thereafter escaped its allure. The "bright shadow" of holiness subsequently drew him God-ward. The medieval artists who painted halos around the heads of Jesus and the saints drew faithful portraits: there is a glow, an allure, to sanctity. Still more, to become what they represent, saintly persons, is humankind's true end.

Admittedly few reach the sanctity of saints such as Francis of Assisi. Nor is our century, it seems, a century of saints! Nor is it, conversely, distinguished by bold, hardened sinners—the Bluebeard-buccaneers of pirate lore. Lamenting the lack of tasty food (sinners) modernity affords, Screwtape declared (in the "Toast" Lewis later appended to *The Screwtape Letters*): "The

94

C. S. LEWIS

great (and toothsome) sinners are made out of the very same
material as those horrible phenomena the great Saints. The virtual disappearance of such material may mean insipid meals
for us. But is it not utter frustration and famine for the Enemy?
He did not create the humans—He did not become one of them
and die among them by torture—in order to produce candi-
dates for Limbo, 'failed' humans. He wanted to make Saints;
gods; things like Himself."[6]

The Way of the Cross is hardly a weekend game of golf.

One senses in Lewis an impatience with the mediocrity that
too often characterizes modern Christendom, a distaste for the
easygoing preaching that neglects or soft-pedals the call to holiness. To him, the gospel surely contains "hard" truths. So he
had little respect for those who would portray the Way of Christ
as a "party." The Way of the Cross is hardly a weekend game of
golf. The kingdom of God is not a cosmic factory outlet mart
that discounts the spiritual disciplines while claiming the "free
gift" of an "abundant life." Christian faith meant far more to
Lewis than being saved "by grace alone through faith alone" (especially in its popular presentations). In his thinking this often
amounts to little more than a friendly nod to Jesus, taking comfort in such diluted definitions of faith as "accepting the fact
that you are accepted."

For Lewis full salvation involves personal transformation.
The end of God's work for us and in us is not merely forgiveness but sanctity. To those (especially in the Reformed tradition)
who believe we are "holy" by virtue of our "position" in Christ,
Lewis would counter that only those who are truly regenerated,
only those who are actually transformed, deserve the label
"Christian." Being "born again" is crucial, for the Christian life
must in fact begin at some point. But the really important issue
is not where or how we begin but where we go and what we
are when we get there! More important than beginning is finishing! Being "born again" is not a momentary "decision" that col-
ors our character with indelible ink, fixing our identity there-

after no matter what we do. It is, rather, the life-changing start of a lifelong change in character, the workings of God's grace conforming us to the nature of Christ. Thus we validate our faith as we "fight the good fight" and "finish the race," becoming truly Christlike. For: "He meant what He said. Those who put themselves in His hands will become perfect, as He is perfect—perfect in love, wisdom, joy, beauty, and immortality."[7]

As the letter to the Hebrews declared: "Wherefore Jesus also, that he might sanctify the people with his own blood, suffered without the gate. Let us go forth therefore unto him without the camp, bearing his reproach. For here have we no continuing city, but we seek one to come" (13:12-14, KJV). So, "Follow peace with all men, and holiness, without which no man shall see the Lord: looking diligently lest any man fail of the grace of God; lest any root of bitterness springing up trouble you, and thereby many be defiled; lest there be any fornicator, or profane person, as Esau, who for one morsel of meat sold his birthright" (12:14-16, KJV).

11 ✐ Perfectly Christian

"The Whole of Christianity"

He never talked vague, idealistic gas. When He said, "Be perfect," He meant it. He meant that we must go in for the full treatment. It is hard; but the sort of compromise we are all hankering after is harder—in fact, it is impossible. It may be hard for an egg to turn into a bird: it would be a jolly sight harder for it to learn to fly while remaining an egg. We are like eggs at present. And you cannot go on indefinitely being just an ordinary, decent egg. We must be hatched or go bad.
May I come back to what I said before? This is the whole of Christianity. There is nothing else.[1]

THOUGH C. S. LEWIS DISLIKED PETTY THEOLOGICAL QUARRELS, noting that "Partisan 'Churchmanships' are my *bete noir*,"[2] he never hesitated to craft careful distinctions, to quickly turn intolerant, when basic truths were at stake. Tolerance, where truth's at stake, becomes treason. His sure-handed grasp of Christian tradition and doctrine, as deft as a seven iron in the hands of a skilled golfer, prompted him to take sides. Standing idly in the grandstands while untruth and heresy wafted through the rotting gauze of moldy minds was not his nature!

Thus his presentation of full salvation encompassed much more than the "justification by faith" views of many Evangelicals. Being "born again" is a glorious launching pad, not a padded couch for lifelong therapy. The temptation to celebrate a grace that cost Christ everything but costs us nothing must be consigned to the doctrinal trash dump. Claiming we're "justified by faith alone" fails to prescribe the full-orbed treatment God has planned for us sinners!

Being "born again" is a glorious launching pad, not a padded couch for lifelong therapy.

The Protestant Reformation sparked by Martin Luther grafted, into the minds of many, a wild apple branch—the conviction that justification by faith alone is the singular standard whereby all else is measured. In response, Anglicans such as C. S. Lewis (and John Wesley before him) emphatically insisted we are saved solely by God's grace, but they refused to tolerate the antinomian tendencies of some "faith alone" advocates. To trumpet a "saved-in-our-sins" *(simul justus et peccatur),* "once saved always saved" gospel, they believed, denies the truly saving reality of God's grace at work in the human heart.

In his fine study of C. S. Lewis, Gilbert Meilander quotes an eminent 20th-century theologian, Anders Nygren, to explain how early and medieval Christian theologians generally envisioned "fellowship with God" as an elevation into, and a partaking of, "God's holiness." Thus *love* rather than *faith* fully unites us with God. Beyond *assenting* to propositional truths concerning Him, we must *act* in accord with the Truth himself, doing His will. "Faith working through love" (Gal. 5:6, RSV) is the surest summary of gospel truth. Through God's grace we can in fact be truly transformed in the depths of our hearts, cooperate with Him so as to fulfill the moral law, and live rightly.

Luther's "Copernican revolution" upended things, Nygren noted, reduced "fellowship with God" to "a fellowship on our human level. Luther's position might be expressed by the formula, *'Fellowship with God on the basis of sin, not of holiness.'"*[3] We're saved, according to this view, because God entered into our predicament as sinners, stooping to our level, sharing our lot—not, as Augustine and others held, because His coming lifts us out of our sins and enables us to live righteously.

Before Luther, medieval Catholics had embraced Augustine's understanding of justification *(iustificare):* "to make righteous." We are justified, "made righteous," as God actually transforms us by His grace. Thus righteousness is *imparted* or infused as well as *imputed,* and God sees us as we are, inwardly cleansed by Christ's blood, not covered by it as if with a Teflon shield. This stance is clearly summed up in the recently issued Catholic Catechism:

> The Paschal mystery has two aspects: by his death Christ liberates us from sin; by his Resurrection, he opens for us the way to a new life. This new life is above all justification that reinstates us in God's grace, "so that as Christ was raised from the dead by the glory of the Father, we too might walk in newness of life."
>
> Justification consists in both victory over the death caused by sin and a new participation in grace.[4]

As in so many other areas, Lewis shared this understanding of salvation that is rooted in the ancient and medieval Church. He emphatically insisted we're united with God on the basis of holiness. As Meilander notes: "For Lewis fellowship with God is, to use Nygren's contrast, on the basis of holiness. His view corresponds quite closely to . . . Augustine's 'caritas synthesis.' The union of the creature with God is fully and entirely the work of grace; yet, it is a union in which the deepest desires of the creature are fulfilled and in which he is cleansed and made fit to dwell in the divine presence."[5]

God's grace enables us to walk with Him, to be holy as He is holy.

In summary, God's grace enables us to walk with Him, to be holy as He is holy, fitted by Him for fellowship with Him. Grace alone—God's loving Spirit within us—transforms us into holy persons. But this grace is not God's self-imposed astigmatism, nor is it a rose-colored lens filtering out our flaws, enabling Him to overlook our continual sinfulness.

The central question is this: are we *declared* righteous or actually *made* righteous? If we believe God *makes* us righteous we must modify the "by faith alone"—*sola fide*—stance of Luther and Calvin. Their position too easily divorces faith and love, demanding faith for salvation while rationalizing the lack of loving acts. To Lewis, as is evident in *The Screwtape Letters,* the devils in hell have a form of "faith," for they "believe" certain truths concerning God. What they lack is love, humility, purity; they refuse to obey and serve Him.

In fact, Scripture clearly calls us to be holy. To imagine God would call us to an impossibility runs counter to His truthfulness! To rightly say we're saved by "grace alone," as Lewis explained, means we are saved by the supernatural, life-changing work of grace in us. We clearly cannot remake ourselves! No self-help manuals, no giddy gurus mouthing candy-coated mantras, no high-priced weekend seminars, can show us shortcuts to holiness. Grace alone—God's loving Spirit within us—transforms us into holy persons. Grace is the costly gift of Christ's cleansing, of full salvation available to all who trust His unfailing love. In Lewis's words: "Now, if I may put it that way, our Lord is like the dentists. If you give Him an inch, He will take an ell. Dozens of people go to Him to be cured of some one particular sin which they are ashamed of (like masturbation or physical cowardice) or which is obviously spoiling daily life (like bad temper or drunkenness). Well, He will cure it all right; but He will not stop there."[6]

God's cure for sin cost Him dearly—and it will cost us as well. We're designed to love God perfectly, and nothing less than a pure heart really can. Nothing less than heart purity prepares us to stand in (and withstand) God's holy presence. As Lewis pictured it: "The Divine Life, which gives itself to us and which calls us to be gods, intends for us something in which morality will be swallowed up. We are to be re-made."[7]

Comparing us, in our sinfulness, with rabbits who need dramatic overhaul, Lewis continues: "All the rabbit in us is to disappear—the worried, conscientious, ethical rabbit as well as the cowardly and sensual rabbit. We shall bleed and squeal as the handfuls of fur come out; and then, surprisingly, we shall find underneath it all a thing we have never yet imagined: a real Man, an ageless god, a son of God, strong, radiant, wise, beautiful, and drenched in joy."[8]

Rigidly Reformed thinkers insist no such "cure" is available in this life, that the only righteousness available to us is "the alien righteousness of Christ" that is imputed to us. Some openly scoff at calls for "Christian perfection." In his radio talks during World War II, brought together in his treatise titled *Mere Christianity,* Lewis acknowledged this difficulty, this "hard saying," noting: "I find a good many people who have been bothered by what I said in the last chapter about our Lord's words, 'Be ye perfect.' Some people seem to think this means 'Unless you are perfect, I will not help you'; and as we cannot be perfect, then, if He meant that, our position is hopeless. But I do not think He did mean that. I think He meant 'The only help I will give is help to become perfect. You may want something less: but I will give you nothing less.'"[9]

Indeed, the real Christian life is a truly satisfying, sanctifying pilgrimage. Lewis expressed this forcefully in a profound passage in *Mere Christianity:* "But what man, in his natural condition, has not got, is Spiritual life—the higher and different sort of life that exists in God." Just as we use "light" and "love" in both physical and spiritual ways, so, too, with the word *life.* In the Greek language, the word *bios* refers to biological life; *zoe* refers to God's gracious gift of spiritual life. Admittedly, there is a certain resemblance between the two kinds of life,

> **but only the sort of resemblance there is between a photo and a place, or a statue and a man. A man who changed from having *Bios* to having *Zoe* would have gone through as big a change as a statue which changed from being a carved stone to being a real man.**
>
> **And that is precisely what Christianity is about. This world is a great sculptor's shop. We are the statues and there is a rumour going round the shop that some of us are some day going to come to life.[10]**

This new life, this necessary casting off the old and putting on the new man, is dramatically detailed in *The Voyage of the Dawn Treader,* one of Lewis's most delightful children's stories. One of the children aboard the *Dawn Treader* was Eustace, a thoroughly nasty and self-centered lad who proved to be a pain to the rest of the ship's crew. On one of the islands they visit, however, Eustace (through sloth and greed) lost his way and was transformed into a dragon, a situation he found utterly distasteful. Finally, after he was sufficiently humbled, Eustace faced the lion Aslan, who told him to remove his dragon skin. He tried, without success, to scratch off his scales, later reporting:

> **Then the lion said—but I don't know if it spoke—You will have to let me undress you. I was afraid of his claws, I can tell you, but I was pretty nearly desperate now. So I just lay flat down on my back and let him do it.**
>
> **The very first tear he made was so deep that I thought it had gone right into my heart. And when he began pulling the skin off, it hurt worse than anything I've ever felt. The only thing that made me able to bear it was just the pleasure of feeling the stuff peel off.**[11]

Submitting to Aslan's will, allowing His claws to surgically remove the hardened skin he could not himself remove, delivered Eustace. To his delight he discovered, when Aslan finally finished with him: "And there was I as smooth and soft as a peeled switch and smaller that I had been. Then he caught hold of me—I didn't like that much for I was very tender underneath now that I'd no skin on—and threw me into the water. It smarted like anything but only for a moment. After that it became perfectly delicious and as soon as I started swimming and splashing I found that all the pain had gone from my arm. And then I saw why. I'd turned into a boy again."[12]

Eustace's transformation, however, had just begun. He was not instantly made whole. Rough edges needed to be sanded smooth. Silly, patently modern illusions instilled by wealthy parents and "progressive" schooling needed to be pulled out like impacted wisdom teeth. Much remained to be done to conform him to God's righteous standard. Eustace certainly "began to be a different boy," but "he had relapses. There were still many days when he could be very tiresome. But most of those I shall not notice. The cure had begun."[13]

Lewis insisted our "spiritual" life begins when we, like Eustace, "voluntarily surrender to Divine grace and become sons of the Heavenly Father in Christ." As Paul explained: "Therefore if any man be in Christ, he is a new creature: old things are passed away; behold, all things are become new. And all things are of God, who hath reconciled us to himself by Jesus Christ, and hath given to us the ministry of reconciliation; to wit, that God was in Christ, reconciling the world unto himself, not imputing their trespasses unto them" (2 Cor. 5:17-19, KJV). As he himself testified: "Not that I have already attained, or am already perfected; but I press on, that I may lay hold of that for which Christ Jesus has also laid hold of me. Brethren, I do not count myself to have apprehended; but one thing I do, forgetting those things which are behind and reaching forward to those things which are ahead, I press toward the goal for the prize of the upward call of God in Christ Jesus" (Phil. 3:12-14, NKJV).

12 Conformed to Christ Jesus

"All Men Were Intended to Be"

In Christ a new kind of man appeared:
and the new kind of life which began in Him
is to be put into us.[1]

The man in Christ rose again: not only the God.
That is the whole point. For the first time
we saw the real man.[2]

It might be said that the regenerate man is
totally different from the unregenerate, for the
regenerate life, the Christ that is formed in him,
transforms every part of him: in it his spirit,
soul and body will all be reborn.[3]

DEEP WITHIN US THERE'S A LONGING—pulsating with the power of our life-instinct—a heart hunger both to be and to be somebody. Few of us gladly embrace, for long, the message that we're worthless chunks of mindless stuff adrift in a cooling cosmos. For deep in our hearts there's a longing, a desire to discover good reason for the honor and respect we feel due us. Leo Tolstoy, the great Russian novelist, powerfully discovered this in middle age. Successful and prosperous, he found nothing truly satisfied his soul. He found himself suddenly asking, continually, "What is it for? What does it lead to?"[4] No answer came from the "authorities" he'd followed. The materialistic science he'd trusted simply urged him to believe he was "a transitory, casual cohesion of particles" without meaning or purpose.[5] At death, the particles disintegrate, the atoms fly into space, and that's all. Yet, Tolstoy found, such "truth" hardly equipped him to face the reality of death!

With Tolstoy, we struggle to find life's design. What were we intended to be? What is our end? Surely we're worth more than atoms and molecules! Thus most of us crave small affirmations (smiles, hugs, compliments) that even minimally reinforce our sense of worth. Unfulfilled in the depths of our being, we resort to verbal games, chanting mantras such as "I'm OK, you're OK," trying like children in dark caverns to dispel our fears with magic spells.

Tragically, the hungers we feel—to be somebody, to discover our dignity, to be loved—often slowly gnaw away like termites at our insides. We're often like darkness-addicted cockroaches, feeding on the world's refuse, fleeing any light that might expose us. Yet even as we hide in the darkness we remember, in subterranean chambers, that we're created in God's image and must somehow regain our lost status as His children.

The gospel thus comes to us who are dead in our trespasses and sins, living in darkness rather than light. In the Good News we not only hear of the Christ who saves us but see in Him what we ultimately should be. We find in Christ—the eternal God's Incarnate Word—a message, a vision, a divinely wrought illustration—whereby we may through faith, transformed by His love, become the "sons of God" we're created to be. "Now the point in Christianity which gives us the greatest shock," Lewis said, "is the statement that by attaching ourselves to Christ, we can 'become Sons of God.'"[6]

> *To share God's life, to be transformed, is to be graciously lifted out of ourselves, to receive a divine life transfusion.*

One of the main themes in Lewis's works, perhaps the primary emphasis wherein one finds his concern for Christian holiness, celebrates the possibility of *transformation,* of actually becoming Christlike, sharing the blessed status of sons of God through the workings of grace. As he said, Christ calls us not to "mere improvement but Transformation."[7] This is possible because the very Son of God, "eternally begotten by His Father" as the creeds declare, assumed human nature. To share God's life, to be transformed, is to be graciously lifted out of ourselves, to receive a divine life transfusion.

Lewis obviously rejected those "cheap grace" versions of "salvation by faith alone" that exclude responsible action, sustained obedience on our part. He taught we're saved by God's grace, saved by the divine working of God in our hearts, and sanctified not by our own endeavors but by submitting to His holy remedies for our salvation. He certainly believed "we are saved by grace, that in our flesh dwells no good thing, that we are, through and through, creatures not creators, derived beings, living not of ourselves but from Christ."[8]

Taking a clue from Aristotle, Lewis thought all genuinely natural longings have real objects that satisfy them. We thirst for water—and water really exists to slake our thirst. We crave physical affection—and people actually exist who touch and hug and caress us. To realize our designed destiny, to satisfy the deepest longings of our hearts, God in mercy through grace grants us what we cannot attain on our own: His life, *eternal life,* something we long for but are naturally unable to attain. When folks honestly examine their deepest hungers, they realize that nothing locked up in the freezer of a cooling earth could possibly satisfy them.

What we most deeply desire is eternal life and the properly purified personalities who are able to enjoy it. It has once and for all been obtained for us by Jesus' Resurrection. As Lewis wrote: "The Man in Christ rose again: not only the God. That is the whole point. For the first time we saw the real man."[9] In our risen Lord we see what man was designed to be: eternally one with God, forever enjoying His holy presence. Lewis never wearied celebrating this truth. We find eternal life only as a gift from God, for as He said: "We are summoned from the outset to combine as creatures with our Creator, as mortals with immortal, as redeemed sinners with sinless Redeemer. His presence, the interaction between Him and us, must always be the overwhelmingly dominant factor in the life we are to lead within the Body, and any conception of Christian fellowship which does not mean primarily fellowship with Him is out of court."[10]

Indeed, as Lewis explains, Christians don't speak of Christ "in them" as if they simply strive to imitate Him. "They mean that Christ is actually operating through them; that the whole mass of Christians are the physical organism through which Christ acts—that we are His fingers and muscles, the cells of His body."[11]

Still more:

> Now the whole offer which Christianity makes is this: that we can, if we let God have His way, come to share in the life of Christ. If we do, we shall then be sharing a life which was begotten, not made, which always has existed and always will exist. Christ is the Son of God. If we share in this kind of life we also shall be sons of God. We shall love the Father as He does and the Holy Ghost will arise in us. He came to this world and became a man in order to spread to other men the kind of life He has—by what I call "good infection." Every Christian is to become a little Christ. The whole purpose of becoming a Christian is simply nothing else.[12]

> *"It is not a change from brainy men to brainier men . . . [it is] from being creatures of God to being sons of God."*

Jesus Christ, the very Word of God, John tells us, is the "true Light, which lighteth every man that cometh into the world" (John 1:9, KJV). And the "light shineth in the darkness; and the darkness comprehended it not" (v. 5, KJV). Jesus actually "came unto his own, and his own received him not" (v. 11, KJV). If we refuse to accept Jesus, we live in sin's darkness. If we live in the darkness, we fail to become what we most deeply want and ought to be. As Lewis declared, we need to step out of ourselves, to cut loose from our ethnic or tribal identities, to actually move beyond our fallen predicament, for "the Christian view is precisely that the Next Step has already appeared. And it is really new. It is not a change from brainy men to brainier men: it is a change that goes off in a totally different direction—a change from being creatures of God to being sons of God. The first instance appeared in Palestine two thousand years ago."[13]

Jesus' good news makes clear that "all who received him, to those who believed in his name, he gave the right to become children of God" (John 1:12). We never find personal dignity, we never become God's children, simply because we're born into, or join, a social group. Our bloodline may be impressive in many ways. We may trace our ancestry back to the Pilgrims on the *Mayflower*, or to those Indians who met them on Plymouth Rock. There's a rightful sense of self-worth that comes from owning and celebrating your forebears. But we're not born into God's kingdom by being born into a certain race or tribe or family, nor do we become God's sons by joining a certain religious group.

One of the central truths acclaimed by various Early Church Fathers such as Irenaeus of Lyons was repeated by Lewis in *Mere Christianity*: "The Son of God became a man to enable men to become sons of God."[14] Indeed: "God became man to turn creatures into sons: not simply to produce better men of the old kind but to produce a new kind of man. It is not like teaching a horse to jump better and better but like turning a horse into a winged creature."[15]

Rather than admit our limitations and turn to God, rather than return home to the Father who designed us, we're tempted to idolize our group, to worship its achievements. For at least two centuries, many people have believed in human ingenuity, hoped for human progress, and lived for the "coming" transformation of society that would insure the physical comfort of all humankind. For some, the power of technology, which places man atop nature, would, decade by decade, make the world a perfect place. Scientific advances, genetic improvements, utopian political designs, all allowed many to think human problems had purely human solutions. Yet the great ideals of socialistic welfare states—making everyone moderately secure and prosperous, even where half-realized—have hardly made people happier and better.

Throughout Lewis's novel *That Hideous Strength,* this theme dominates: our effort to transform ourselves leads to the death and destruction that comes to the National Institute for Co-ordinated Experiments. One of the N.I.C.E. scientists, Philostrato, longs to create a world "free of Nature," lacking all vegetation and organic life. As he envisioned it, the institute existed "for the conquest of death: or for the conquest of organic life, if you prefer," to manufacture "the artificial man, free from Nature," who totally controls the planet.[16] Much like some who now argue for "cloning" human beings, Philostrato sought to escape the limits of nature, to secure an eternal life totally subject to man.

In fact, Lewis taught, it's only if we follow the example of the St. Anne's community, standing against N.I.C.E. in *That Hideous Strength,* that we attain our end. We become holy, not through our own efforts, but through the supernatural workings of the Holy Spirit and the appointed "means of grace" granted us. Rather than tacking them together to construct a utopian world, rather than gluing together political factions to secure "peace and prosperity," rather than ratcheting up economic programs and social reforms, we must relax and accept the good gifts available to us here and now.

The contrast drawn between the secular, scientific crowd at N.I.C.E. and the religious folks at St. Anne's was finally noted by Mark, the young sociologist. As he determined to return to his wife, Jane, who had joined the community St. Anne's, he pondered his own discontent with life. He wondered how the good folks there wandered

> **through the world with all their muscles relaxed and a careless eye roving the horizon, bubbling over with fancy and humour, sensitive to beauty, not continually on their guard and not needing to be. What was the secret of that fine, easy laughter which he could not by any efforts imitate? Everything about them was different. They could not even fling themselves into**

chairs without indolence. There was elbow-room in
their lives, as there had never been in his. They were
Hearts: he was only a Spade.[17]

The secret to all this good humor, the lordliness, the elbow
room Mark sensed in St. Anne's, lay in the *holiness* of the folks
who lived there—a holiness derived from their cheerful submission to the guidance of Elwin Ransom. Following his instructions, they cooperated with the Eldils (angels) whose supernatural presence assisted the community. The spirits' presence at
St. Anne's may be likened to the Spirit's presence in the Christian life, transforming and sanctifying Christ's disciples amid
the ordinary routines of life. And consequently we're enabled to
become all we're meant to be.

> *The gospel, the good news that*
> *Jesus Christ became man, tells us*
> *that God became man, . . . that God*
> *has taken the initiative and seeks*
> *to give us the life that we lost.*

In Adam's fall, in the continued apostasy of Adam's kin, we
live physically but not spiritually. The Bible declares we are
dead in our trespasses and sins. The most precious of goods
eludes us, for we're unable on our own to regain the spiritual
life that was lost in Eden. But the gospel, the good news that Jesus Christ became man, tells us that God has taken the initiative
and seeks to give us that life, that *zoe,* which we lost. It's solely
through His grace—the grace that is Jesus Christ, the living
Word of God—that we become the person God designed us to
be. If we give up on our self-help programs, if we confess our
spiritual poverty, we'll find grace available that will impart to us
His divine life.

As Paul declared:

For we ourselves also were sometimes foolish, disobe-
dient, deceived, serving divers lusts and pleasures, living

in malice and envy, hateful, and hating one another. But after that the kindness and love of God our Saviour toward man appeared, not by works of righteousness which we have done, but according to his mercy he saved us, by the washing of regeneration, and renewing of the Holy Ghost; which he shed on us abundantly through Jesus Christ our Saviour; that being justified by his grace, we should be made heirs according to the hope of eternal life *(Titus 3:3-7, KJV).*

Purity of Heart Is to Will One Thing

13   Put On the New Man

"An Alteration of the Will"
"Die Before You Die"

A repentance and renewal of what the other side call "grace" on the scale which you describe is a defeat of the first order. It amounts to a second conversion—and probably on a deeper level than the first.[1]

Conversion requires an alteration of the will, and an alteration which, in the last resort, does not occur without the intervention of the supernatural.[2]

SOMETHING IN US LONGS FOR FRESH STARTS, new beginnings. One reason I enjoy teaching is because twice a year I get another chance to teach an old course—such as ethics—facing a new group of students. Without fail, I hope to finally do it right! At the beginning of each term, the classroom is packed. Zealous youngsters ask to "crash" the course, pushing the enrollment beyond its official limit. My students and I throb with anticipation, excitement, planning to master the subject and maximize our potential. Four months later, however, we're all exhausted, hoping to somehow make it through, feeling a bit battered and scarred, thankful to have accomplished something less than we'd hoped. Yet in a few days, after a short break, we're ready for a new term—and the possibility of attaining what we know we're capable of.

What's true for a college class is equally true for life. Things never seem to go quite as they should, so we think we'd do better if only we could start over! As Erma Bombeck titled one of her books: *The Grass Is Always Greener over the Septic Tank!* If only some things were different. Still more deeply: if only we could be someone other than we are! As Queen Orual noted, in Lewis's *Till We Have Faces,* "We have all had our dream of some other land, some other world, some other way of giving prizes which would bring us in as the conquerors."[3]

> ## *If only Adam and Eve had refused to nibble at the lure Satan dangled before them.*

Indeed, we sense that we'd be better off if only Adam and Eve had obeyed God and humbly embraced their status as His creatures; if only they'd preserved their original holiness, their true design; if only they'd actually resisted Satan's assault, refused to nibble at the lure he dangled before them; if only they'd acted differently! We know, as a consequence, that we're less than we're designed to be, less than we're capable of being. So we feel guilty, not simply for things we do but for failing to be what we know we should be.

Till We Have Faces, one of Lewis's finest novels, tells the story of Orual, a pagan queen of the ancient kingdom of Glome. Sour and angry as life's final curtain fell, she wrote a detailed denunciation of the gods. She blamed them for all her pain and suffering, most especially the loss of her sister, Psyche, who in the flower of her youth had been sacrificed to atone for Glome's sins. Then the story unexpectedly shifts, and the novel's closing section details the dreams and visions that came to Orual, prompted by the memories roused in the process of writing her book that unexpectedly prepared her for the "gods' surgery."[4] She at last saw herself as she was: a woman whose life had been consumed by jealousy and hate, cleverly disguised as "love" for her lost sister. As she faced this painful truth, "those divine Surgeons had me tied down and were at work. My anger protected me only for a short time; anger wearies itself out and truth comes in."[5]

An arrogant self-will, an inflated self-esteem, easily rules where it should serve.

So she removed the veil she'd worn all her adult life to hide her deformed face and walked about barefaced. She finally dared to reveal herself and in that act opened her soul to the gods she'd attempted to deny. She heard a voice that said: "Die before you die. There is no chance after."[6] She'd heard the same voice as a child, and it "had not changed in all those years, but I had. There was no rebel in me now."[7] She was, for the first time, ready to change. She realized that an arrogant self-will, an inflated self-esteem, easily rules where it should serve. To submit, to serve, is to die to the tyrant self.

Orual had, early in life, donned a veil to cover her "ugly" face, but the real ugliness was in her heart. After 40 years of self-deceit, she had to admit the truth, confess her sins, allow that the gods were in fact real and right in their ways. In a culminating vision, she ventured into the mountains where the gods lived and voiced her complaints to the judge, especially lamenting the loss of Psyche. "The girl was mine," she pouted. "What right had you to steal her away into your dreadful heights? You'll say I was jealous. Jealous of Psyche? Not while she was mine."[8] But the gods took her! So, Orual insisted, "There's no room for you and us in the same world. You're a tree in whose shadow we can't thrive. We want to be our own. I was my own and Psyche was mine and no one else had any right to her."[9]

What Orual discovered in her vision was that "the complaint was the answer."[10] "I saw well why the gods do not speak to us openly, nor let us answer. Till that word can be dug out of us, why should they hear the babble that we think we mean? How can they meet us face to face till we have faces?"[11] Then, as she confessed her transgressions, admitting her selfish attitudes and misguided acts, she found herself now ready to join Psyche in worshiping the true god. As he came, "The air was growing brighter and brighter about us; as if something had set it on fire. Each breath I drew led me into new terror, joy, overpowering sweetness. I was pierced through and through with the arrows of it. I was being unmade. I was no one."[12]

According to Lewis, to be "unmade," to "die before you die," is the deepest secret unveiled to us, the true clue to discerning life's mystery. Following this divinely given vision, Orual regained consciousness. Approaching death, she wrote: "I ended my first book with the words no answer. I know now, Lord, why you utter no answer. You are yourself the answer."[13] We need not so much new truths or more moving experiences. Rather we need a Real Presence, a Divine Person: the Truth. At the last moment, Orual turned to God. In submission, like a sheet laid out on an ironing board, she allowed a stronger hand to smooth out the wrinkles of that bent to evil that had turned her away from God. In humility, she placed her life back in His hands.

The "small" decisions, the things we do day by day, often deeply dye our character.

One of the fundamental themes of *Till We Have Faces* is human freedom. In her desire to live freely, to take charge of her own destiny, Orual failed, for true freedom comes only through total surrender to God's will. Throughout his many works, C. S. Lewis continually emphasized the eternal significance of our decisions, willful acts, commitments. Often these are "small" decisions, the things we do day by day that deeply dye our character. Real repentance, turning over oneself to God, involves the will, freely surrendering the pretense of self-sovereignty to embrace the reality of God's sovereignty.

In the second volume of his space trilogy, *Perelandra,* Lewis describes Elwin Ransom's journey to the planet Perelandra (Venus) and of his role, representing Maleldil (Christ), helping the "Green Lady" resist the temptations of the evil physicist,

Weston, the Un-man. In the midst of a riveting temptation scene, Ransom realized that "his journey to Perelandra was not a moral exercise, nor a sham fight. If the issue lay in Maleldil's hands, Ransom and the Lady were those hands. The fate of a world really depended on how they behaved in the next few hours. The thing was irreducibly, nakedly real. They could, if they chose, decline to save the innocence of this new race, and if they declined its innocence would not be saved."[14]

At first glance, it seemed absurd to Ransom, a scholarly philologist, that Maleldil (the Lord of the new world) would leave the fate of his creation in a creature's hands. Why should such a momentous issue "finally and absolutely depend on such a man of straw as himself?"[15] But then he remembered the world-altering impact of men such as ancient Rome's Horatius at the bridge, or the young Constantine choosing to conquer under the banner of the Cross. Free individuals, singular acts, for better or worse, alter human history. And he remembered the result of Eve's decision in the Garden. "Thus, and not otherwise, the world was made. Either something or nothing must depend on individual choices. And if something, who could set bounds to it? A stone may determine the course of a river. He was that stone at this horrible moment which had become the centre of the whole universe. The eldila of all worlds, the sinless organisms of everlasting light, were silent in Deep Heaven to see what Elwin Ransom of Cambridge would do."[16]

In the midst of his struggle, Ransom suddenly realized that all he needed to do was "to do his best." Whether or not he could defeat the powers of evil he knew not. But he had to take a stand and engage Weston in combat. "Here in Perelandra the temptation would be stopped by Ransom, or it would not be stopped at all."[17] It helped, mustering up the courage to face his fears, when he remembered a few times earlier in his life when he'd done what seemed "impossible."

Despite his scholarly temperament, his reluctance to do physical combat, he realized that Weston's body was the only outpost for evil in Perelandra. It must be destroyed. Something good, however small, had to be done. He'd done it before. He could do it again. Once he'd decided this, when he'd finally fixed his will, the future act was in fact determined. The strug-

gle in his heart ended. The struggle with Weston had not yet begun—but the real issue had been resolved in Ransom's surrender to the will of Maleldil.

God's work of full salvation unfolds within us as we decide,
as we set our will, to embrace His truth and submit to His will.
To be holy we need sanctifying truth. And that's exactly what
Jesus offers us. Clearly Christ aims to make us eternally blessed
by making us good here and now. His goodness comes to us as
we are joined to Him. To be fully converted takes more than a
momentary decision to accept His gracious forgiveness. It takes
a deeper work, "an alteration of the will" that "does not occur
without the intervention of the supernatural."[18]

> ## When we "die before we die," we experience the depths of God's gracious workings within us.

When we, like Orual, undergo God's "surgery," when we
"die before we die," we experience the depths of God's gracious
workings within us. So what I really need to know is the truth
about my inner being. Who am I . . . really? If I look to Jesus, if I
listen to Him, He tells me truth about myself. It's not always the
truth I want to hear, but it's the truth that saves and sanctifies. If
I know God seeks to remold me in Christ's image, then I know
I'll be free at last when I allow Him to conform me to that Model. As Lewis said: "The happiness which God designs for His
higher creatures is the happiness of being freely, voluntarily
united to Him and to each other in an ecstasy of love and delight compared with which the most rapturous love between a
man and a woman on this earth is mere milk and water."[19]

Or, as Paul put it: "I beseech you therefore, brethren, by the
mercies of God, that ye present your bodies a living sacrifice,
holy, acceptable unto God, which is your reasonable service. And
be not conformed to this world: but be ye transformed by the renewing of your mind, that ye may prove what is that good, and
acceptable, and perfect, will of God" (Rom. 12:1-2, KJV).

14   Perfect Submission

"Give Me All"

Christ says, "Give me All. I don't want so much of your time and so much of your money and so much of your work: I want You. I have not come to torment your natural self, but to kill it. No half-measures are any good. I don't want to cut off a branch here and a branch there, I want to have the whole tree down."[1]

For the Supernatural, entering a human soul, opens to it new possibilities both of good and evil. From that point the road branches: one way to sanctity, humility, the other to spiritual pride, self-righteousness, persecuting zeal. And no way back to the mere humdrum virtues of the unawakened soul. If the Divine call does not make us better, it will make us very much worse. Of all bad men religious bad men are the worst.[2]

WHEN I ENTERED GRADUATE SCHOOL at the University of Oklahoma in 1963, the football team was, for a while, ranked number one in the nation and featured one of the nation's premier running backs, Joe Don Looney. When he began playing for OU, journalists touted him as a sure All-American, a probable Heisman Memorial Trophy winner. It seemed certain he would soon make his mark in the NFL. Fame and fortune beckoned. He had it all!

But Joe Don Looney never realized his potential. He even failed to finish college. Coach Bud Wilkinson kicked him off the team after he slugged a coach in a practice session. Joe Don, ever the spoiled child, disdained orders, detested instruction, and disregarded the needs of the team. He demanded to play his own game. He'd cut out his own pattern for life, and it led him to arrests for public drunkenness, fights throughout the city of Norman, shouting matches with professors and coaches. Ultimately not even his athletic ability saved him. He lost his scholarship, his collegiate career. When he tried out for some National Football League teams, he never lasted, never became the "star" he imagined he'd be. He self-destructed through self-indulgence.

Looney failed—as some of us will fail—not through lack of ability, but through lack of humility. For the greatest thing our parents can teach us, the greatest thing our teachers can model, the greatest lesson we'll ever master, is the self-discipline that results from learning to obey, accepting others' instructions, yielding to our elders, surrendering to God. It's similar to what Friedrich Nietzsche observed, saying: "The essential thing 'in heaven and earth' is . . . that there should be long obedience in the same direction; there thereby results, and has always resulted in the long run, something which has made life worth living."[3]

> *We've entered a time-tested training facility, where a determined Coach intends to make us the very best athletes He can.*

Though Nietzsche himself never modeled his insight and proudly disdained humility, there is an obedience to humility that begins with confessing our needs, admitting our faults and failures, opening up to God in ways most sinners prefer to avoid. Many of us would like God to massage away some of our minor discomforts, to erase some of our shameful memories, to give us a facelift to make us a bit more presentable. But when we ask Him into our lives, He wants to take charge of our entire being, to make us all we're designed to be—perfect in every way! As Lewis said: "That is why He warned people to 'count the cost' before becoming Christians. 'Make no mistake,' He says, 'if you let me, I will make you perfect. The moment you put yourself in My hands, that is what you are in for. Nothing less, or other, than that. You have free will, and if you choose, you can push Me away. But if you do not push Me away, understand that I am going to see this job through.'"[4]

We've not hired on in the business firm of a softhearted uncle who grants us loans and preferences as well as lifetime security because of his sense of "kin." Rather, we've entered a time-tested training facility, where a determined Coach intends to make us the very best athletes He can. So: "Whatever suffering it may cost you in your earthly life, whatever inconceivable purification it may cost you after death, whatever it costs Me, I will never rest, nor let you rest, until you are literally perfect— until my Father can say without reservation that He is well pleased with you, as He said He was well pleased with Me."[5]

This truth we'd often like to avoid. Addicted to sins of various sorts, we'd rather have another cup of coffee, eat another ice cream cone, sleep another hour, do anything but accept God's solution to our heart's needs. We'd often like to pick up some of God's blessings—like ecstatic winners of TV game show contests—but not go daily to the weight rooms and struggle to develop our muscles, to allow His blessed sanctifying work in our souls. Nor would we like to admit our limits, our inability to live life well on our own. Deep in our hearts, many of us would like to be *the answer man* or *the messiah*. Yet Scripture ever reminds us that we're called to a humility that rejects such pretenses!

Such saving humility gains clarity in *The Horse and His Boy,* one of *The Chronicles of Narnia.* Fleeing from Calormen slavery, two horses, Bree and Hwin, and their riders, Aravis and Shasta, seek freedom in the North, the good land of Narnia. Amid their adventures they encounter, and are helped by, some subtle moves by the lion Aslan. As the story ends, they finally see him in his fullness, his splendor. Fear overwhelms them. Lions, of course, occasionally eat horses! After a tense moment,

Hwin, though shaking all over, gave a strange little neigh, and trotted across to the Lion.

"Please," she said, "you're so beautiful. You may eat me if you like. I'd sooner be eaten by you than fed by anyone else."

"Dearest daughter," said Aslan, planting a lion's kiss on her twitching, velvet nose, "I knew you would not be long in coming to me. Joy shall be yours."[6]

Hwin's humility, presenting her body "a living sacrifice" (Rom. 12:1, KJV) to Aslan, was the key decision in her life. Her companion, Bree, still hesitated, so Aslan

lifted his head and spoke in a louder voice.

"Now Bree," he said, "you poor, proud, frightened Horse, draw near. Nearer still, my son. Do not dare not to dare. Touch me. Smell me. Here are my paws, here is my tail, these are my whiskers. I am a true Beast."

"Aslan," said Bree in a shaken voice, "I'm afraid I must be rather a fool."

"Happy the horse who knows that while he is still young. Or the Human either."[7]

Clearly there are times when to be a "fool" for Christ—to have "childlike faith," to "blindly" leap into the unknown realms of God's will, to abandon the pretense that we're someone other than we really are—brings us into the sanctifying presence of Christ. "But there must be a real giving up of the self. You must throw it away 'blindly' so to speak. Christ will indeed give you a real personality: but you must not go to Him for the sake of that. As long as your own personality is what you are bothering about you are not going to Him at all. The very first step is to try to forget about the self altogether."[8]

> ## Through sustained surrender, allowing Christ to guide us, we discover the secret of holy living.

Forgetting self enables us to acknowledge what's ultimately crucial: that "Christ lives in us." We can, both at a decisive beginning point of complete consecration and in subsequent reaffirmations of that act, die to the "old man," the "false self," the alien tyrant who pretends to know how we should live. Through sustained surrender, turning loose and keeping our hands free from the steering wheel of our life, allowing Christ to guide us, we discover the secret of holy living.

Beyond admitting our need of God we must submit to instruction, submit to discipline, surrendering our deepest self to God. As Lewis said:

> **The principle runs through life from top to bottom. Give up yourself, and you will find your real self. Lose your life and you will save it. Submit to death, death of your ambitions and favourite wishes every day and death of your whole body in the end: submit with every fibre of your being, and you will find eternal life. Keep nothing back. Nothing that you have not given away will ever be really yours. Nothing that has not died will ever be raised from the dead.[9]**

That's what the horses Bree and Hwin discovered as they entered Narnia's safe harbor. Giving up, submitting to the will of Aslan, was necessary in order to become the horses they longed to be. Losing themselves, they found their real selves.

There's wisdom in committing one's whole being to something better and wiser than oneself.

In admitting we need help, in submitting to God's guidance, we can then commit our lives to Him, serving Him in joy. There's wisdom in committing one's whole being to something better and wiser than oneself. One of the main characters in *That Hideous Strength,* Jane, discovered this. She'd tried to live in her own strength, resisting any efforts of her husband, Mark, or anyone else to impose their will on her. But life turned chaotic as Mark was swept into the N.I.C.E. circle of evil, and Jane was mysteriously drawn to the peaceful, hierarchically ordered, Christian community of St. Anne's.

At first she resisted joining the group, for she was told, "If you don't give yourself to us, the enemy will use you."[10] "The words, 'give yourself to us,' were ill-chosen. The very muscles of Jane's body stiffened a little."[11] She'd never fully given "herself" to anyone! Even worse, she was actually told to get husband Mark's "permission" before joining St. Anne's. That made her absolutely angry! She was, after all, a "modern," liberated woman, utterly freed from such old-fashioned notions as "obeying" one's husband!

Jane had, in fact, always sought individual autonomy. She sought to dictate the terms, to specify the conditions, of her life's contract. So she'd entered marriage, rather like a business deal, assuming it was a contract with clear provisions rather than an unconditional covenant. She wanted a husband, but she resisted any other person's authority over her. "Though she did not formulate it, this fear of being invaded and entangled was the deepest ground of her determination not to have a child—or not for a long time yet. One had one's own life to live."[12]

Only later, having watched her world collapse, having been physically tortured by "Fairy" (the sadistic, perverted, lesbian head of the N.I.C.E. police force), did Jane flee to St. Anne's. There she learned from Ransom, the community's "Director," the ancient truth "'that you do not fail in obedience through lack of love, but have lost love because you never attempted obedience.'"[13] Her unhappy marriage, her unhappiness with herself, stemmed from her lack of humility, her stubborn refusal to submit to anyone other than herself.

Her attitude has recently come to the foreground, lifted to a flag as an admirable stance, in certain feminist circles. For example, Daphne Hampson urges modern women to redefine sin: "Woman's 'sin' is—to quote an effective phrase of Judith Plaskow's—'the failure to take responsibility for self-actualization.' To name such behaviour 'sin' is . . . very effective. For women to hear that it is their right and duty to take themselves seriously, that it matters who they are and what they think, is to turn Christian theology as they have imbibed it upside-down."[14] Women, Hampson declares, have been taught to be humble and "self-effacing," to sacrifice themselves for the good of others, destroying themselves in the process. They need to reject such attitudes and commit themselves to self-assertion.

What Jane discovered was precisely what gender feminists such as Hampson deny: nothing satisfies the soul quite so much as self-sacrifice. Thus, having foundered while following her own "self-realization" schemes, she found in Ransom's strangely warm yet demanding presence, a patriarchal love she'd long resisted, "instantly her world was unmade."[15] "For the first time in all those years she tasted the word King itself with all linked associations of battle, marriage, priesthood, mercy, and power. At that moment, as her eyes first rested on his face, Jane forgot who she was, and where, and her faint grudge against Grace Ironwood, and her more obscure grudge against Mark, and her childhood and her father's house. It was, of course, only for a flash. . . . But her world was unmade; she knew that. Anything might happen now."[16]

Strangely enough, "At the very moment when her mind was most filled with another man [Ransom], there arose, clouded with some undefined emotion, a resolution to give Mark much more than she had ever given him before, and a feeling that in so doing she would be really giving it to the Director."[17]

If we ever commit all we are to God, we find the freedom to relax, the grace that gives us peace. In a stressed-out world, we find the wisdom to live stress-free. For we can relax when we're content with our lot in life, with the assignment we've been given, rather than demanding the role we imagine is right for us. Such relaxed humility may surprise us, for it's often strong and self-confident, close to what Aristotle admired in "high-minded" persons. Lewis explained that a truly humble person is not "what most people call 'humble' nowadays; he will not be a sort of greasy, smarmy person, who is always telling you that, of course, he is nobody. Probably all you will think about him is that he seemed a cheerful, intelligent chap who took a real interest in what you said to him. If you do dislike him it will be because you feel a little envious of anyone who seems to enjoy life so easily. He will not be thinking about humility: he will not be thinking about himself at all."[18]

There's much wisdom in what I call the *wu wei way*. The Chinese philosopher Lao-tzu urged readers to follow *wu wei*—the flow of things, fitting into the way things are. It's like canoeing whitewater streams in the Ozark Mountains. Skillful paddlers use a few judicious strokes to keep the canoe in the swift-flowing channel of the stream's current, speeding past those who try to muscle their crafts downstream with furious action. To "go with the flow" sometimes means drifting aimlessly, but when canoeing it accurately describes using a stream's current to attain one's end.

> ## *By flowing with the divine current, not by making our own way, we wisely navigate life.*

In the stresses of life there's a divine current—the will of God. By flowing with that current, not by making our own way, we wisely navigate life. This navigation enables us to play our assigned "role," to assume our "position," in the pageant of life. This approach enables us to gracefully, gratefully embrace our "gifts" and exercise them in the Body of Christ, cheerfully applauding those who get more attention than ourselves, cheerfully accepting responsibilities and tasks that demand work and sacrifice. That's the humility that admits its needs, submits to God's will, and commits itself to the task of living freely and responsibly in our world.

At this level of self-surrender God sanctifies us holy. Jesus meant it when He said, "Give me all." For God wants to cut down the "whole tree" of our self-reliant pretense, and He will not stop with chopping away a few branches here and there. Thus John the Baptist envisioned Jesus' mission: "I indeed baptize you with water unto repentance: but he that cometh after me is mightier than I, whose shoes I am not worthy to bear: he shall baptize you with the Holy Ghost, and with fire: whose fan is in his hand, and he will throughly purge his floor, and gather his wheat into the garner; but he will burn up the chaff with unquenchable fire" (Matt. 3:11-12, KJV).

15 ✍ All to Jesus
I Surrender

"The Key to All Doors"

Obedience is the key to all doors; feelings come (or don't come) and go as God pleases. We can't produce them at will, and mustn't try.[1]

Milton was right: . . . The choice of every lost soul can be expressed in the words "Better to reign in Hell than serve in Heaven."[2]

I'M OFTEN HAUNTED BY THE TITLE of Professor Neal Postman's book *Amusing Ourselves to Death.* He argues that the best symbol for modern America is Las Vegas, Nevada, a city humming with frantic people, continuously aglow with the glare of neon signs, devoted to letting the good times roll! With Frank Sinatra, folks sing "I did it my way"—the probable lyrics, Peter Kreeft notes, of hell's theme song! Doing it "my way," doing what "feels good," rather typifies our age. Consequently, we're literally killing ourselves with multiplied addictions, amusements, and diversions—many of which are devised to numb our souls and keep us distracted from eternal concerns.

To a degree I understand how secular worldlings embrace the ancient injunction: "Let us eat, drink, and be merry, for tomorrow we shall die." I'm less able to understand, however, how such an attitude slips like a cat burglar into the Church of Jesus Christ. Yet we often tailor our message and orchestrate our worship services to entertain and amuse. "Let the good times roll!" we suggest in "worship" services that allegedly attribute "worth" to God. "Come to Jesus," we too often plead, assuring folks that Christ will make us successful, insure our comfort, add a bulge to our bank account, hit the jackpot of life! Unfortunately, it's just not true!

I was prodded to think about this years ago when, in a chapel talk at MidAmerica Nazarene College (now MidAmerica Nazarene University), Jimmy Dobson (father of the "Focus on the Family" founder Dr. James Dobson) recounted his first experience as a pastor. Having graduated from Bethany Peniel College (now Southern Nazarene University), Dobson went to a little church in a beat-up town in Louisiana. Fortified by his reading of holiness "classics," filled with advice from college professors, confident his sincerity would make for a "successful" ministry, he assumed that enough hard work, diligent prayer, faith, and anointed preaching would revive that little church and ignite a blaze of spiritual glory in the town.

The opposite, however, happened. Week by week, month by month, the little crowd withered away like drought-dried cornstalks. The more he worked, the less folks cared or came. The more he prayed, the less "spiritual" he felt. To make matters worse, his little boy (the now famous James) took sick, so he and his mother had to go to her folks' place for medical aid. For several months, Jimmy Dobson lived alone, certain he had utterly failed, wondering if he'd been called to preach, wondering at God's ways with His servants.

God is less concerned with our success than with our holiness.

What Dobson discovered, and what we must discover as we mature in our walk with God, is that God is less concerned with our success than with our holiness. We discover, in life's dark times, that we really need to wholly surrender our whole self to the holy will of God. We find, as C. S. Lewis observed in one of his most profound passages, that "there are only two kinds of people in the end: those who say to God, 'Thy will be done,' and those to whom God says, in the end, 'Thy will be done.' All that are in Hell, choose it. Without that self-choice there could be no Hell. No soul that seriously and constantly desires joy will ever miss it. Those who seek find. To those who knock it is opened."[3]

There's really no third option, no middle ground. This means, Lewis noted, that: "Milton was right: . . . The choice of every lost soul can be expressed in the words 'Better to reign in Hell than serve in Heaven.'"[4] Conversely, those who enjoy heaven forever gladly choose to serve.

Thus it's a choice with eternal consequences. Some, disobeying God, choose hell. However we might like to avoid it, the Bible—and especially Jesus himself—stress the everlasting reality of damnation. As Lewis explained:

> **If a game is played, it must be possible to lose it. If the happiness of a creature lies in self-surrender, no one can make that surrender but himself (though many can help him to make it) and he may refuse. I would pay any price to able to say truthfully "All will be saved," but my reason retorts, "Without their will, or with it?" If I say "Without their will" I at once perceive a contradiction; how can the supreme voluntary act of self-surrender be involuntary?[5]**

On the night before He was crucified, Jesus struggled with His Father's will in Gethsemane's garden. While His disciples waited—and slept—Jesus prayed for deliverance. He clearly felt an anguish that shook Him to the depths of His being. Repeatedly He prayed: "O my Father, if it be possible, let this cup pass from me: nevertheless not as I will, but as thou wilt" (Matt. 26:39, KJV). In Gethsemane Jesus demonstrated the reality of His Incarnation. Fully God, He became fully man and experienced in that union with us all that we experience. He lived with all the anxieties that trouble us, haunt us, inwardly devour us. He knew the anguished awareness of our perplexities regarding the future. In Jesus, the God-man, we see illustrated perfect obedience. In Gethsemane, we see Him, as fully human as any of us, suffering, struggling with His Father's will for the future.

Most of us struggle when facing uncertainties, the insecurities of an unknown future. We'd like to know things are nailed down, safe, beyond destruction. The central characters in *Pere-*

landra, Elwin Ransom and the Green Lady, struggled similarly. The temptation was to seek the security of the "Fixed Land" rather than accept the fluid ebb and flow of the water and islands on which they were placed. Toward the end of the book, the Lady declared her mind had been confused by the "Evil One." After Ransom killed the Un-man, Weston, she understood that her desire to live on the "Fixed Land" had been a temptation to defy God. "It was to reject the wave—to draw my hands out of Maleldil's, to say to Him, 'Not thus, but thus'—to put in our own power what times should roll towards us . . . as if you gathered fruits together to-day for to-morrow's eating instead of taking what came. That would have been cold love and feeble trust. And out of it how could we ever have climbed back into love and trust again?"[6]

> *I've discovered . . . God's will is not narrowly restricted to what I do. Rather, it's focused on the kind of* person *I become in the process of what I do.*

We often think we'd like a road map, a precise blueprint for the future, placed in our hands by an all-knowing God. Yet God seems to give us little more than a few terse instructions, along with a few sharp reproofs as we journey! In fact, life's more enjoyable when we live with expectancy, awaiting its adventures. And I've discovered that God's will is not narrowly restricted to what I *do.* Rather, it's focused on the kind of *person* I become in the process of whatever it is that I do. The divine Potter has designs: He wants to make us better. Yet He'll not take the lump of clay and create a beautiful vessel without its assent. Only as we surrender to Him, only as we obey as servants, do we find ourselves transformed into His sons.

In one of the Narnian chronicles, *The Silver Chair,* Aslan sends forth Eustace and Jill to rescue Prince Rilian, who had been captured by the evil witch, the Queen of Underland. He sent them with a minimum of mysterious instructions—four signs. They couldn't fathom their meaning. They made no more sense than sign language to folks who've never learned it. But they were entrusted with them, much as a diplomatic courier is commissioned to carry a top-secret message. On the final leg of their journey, they were trapped in the depths of an underground chamber, from which they thought they might never escape. At that point, the Marsh-wiggle Puddleglum simply declared: "You see, Aslan didn't tell [Jill] Pole what would happen. He only told her what to do. That fellow will be the death of us once he's up. I shouldn't wonder. But that doesn't let us off following the Sign."[7]

Obeying God is ultimately more like a dance than drudgery.

As Lewis explains: "Now the proper good of a creature is to surrender itself to its Creator—to enact intellectually, volitionally, and emotionally, that relationship which is given in the mere fact of its being a creature. When it does so, it is good and happy."[8] This is the "obedience" that characterizes the Son's love for the Father. It is the "obedience" Adam and Eve disdained, bringing sin into all our race. It is the "obedience" that will swell all of heaven with the joy of the saints who have found its secret. So, Lewis continued: "In the world as we know it, the problem is how to recover this self-surrender. We are not merely imperfect creatures who must be improved: we are, as Newman said, rebels who must lay down our arms."[9] This we hate to do! This above all we resist, for we're bona fide rebels! Obedience threatens our illusions, punctures all our pretenses. That's because "to surrender a self-will inflamed and swollen with years of usurpation is a kind of death. We all remember this self-will as it was in childhood, the bitter, prolonged rage at every thwarting, the burst of passionate tears, the black, Satanic wish to kill or die rather than to give in. Hence the older type of nurse or parent was quite right in thinking that the first step in education is 'to break the child's will.'"[10]

To "break" our will sounds, to modern ears, harsh and love-less. But in fact, since love *wills* the good of the beloved, there's no higher love, no nobler aspiration, than God's absolute, un-remitting resolve to free us from the tyranny of self-will. For if only we obey Him we'll find His healing remedy at work within us. Obeying God, as is evident in *That Hideous Strength,* is ulti-mately more like a dance than drudgery. In a revealing conver-sation with the Director (Ransom), Jane was mildly shocked to see him take a plate and tip it, spilling the bread crumbs on the floor. Then he blew a little silver whistle, and three mice ap-peared! Ordinarily she'd have been repelled by mice, but now she saw them in a new, truer light. The little creatures solemnly made their way across the carpet and began cleaning up the crumbs. When they'd finished their work, the Director blew the whistle again and the mice dashed back to their home in the wall. "'There,' he said, 'a very simple adjustment. Humans want crumbs removed; mice are anxious to remove them. It ought never to have been a cause of war. But you see that obe-dience and rule are more like a dance than a drill—specially be-tween man and woman where the roles are always changing.'"[11]

Like the mice, we're called to obey, to join the cosmic dance, to join in the eternally loving communion that characterizes the Holy Trinity, the co-inherence of divine fellowship. Like me-dieval knights, pledging fealty to their lord, moving to the music of chivalry's code, we choose the obedience that leads to joy. Thus: "Obedience is the road to freedom, humility the road to pleasure, unity the road to personality."[12]

> *Surrendering completely to God's will gives us the key to living the Christlike life.*

Often, when I need some spiritual solace, I play "soul gospel" records. One of my favorites was recorded years ago by the Beautiful Mount Zion Missionary Baptist Church in Chicago. One song, the rendering of an old text, always touches me. A soaring woman's voice sings:

I need Jesus, as I walk this narrow way, this narrow way,
He will guide my faltering footsteps, as I travel day-by-day,
    where my God leads me,
For I know He knows the way,
And I cannot, no I cannot, make the journey, all by myself.

Confessing "I need Jesus," recognizing we cannot endure the pains and injustices of life in our own strength, surrendering completely to God's will, gives us the key to living the Christlike life. It's Christ's key, the Gethsemane key, minted on the Mount of Olives, the sacred space where we need to yield our all to God. As Luke recorded: "And he was withdrawn from them about a stone's cast, and kneeled down, and prayed, saying, Father, if thou be willing, remove this cup from me: nevertheless not my will, but thine, be done" (Luke 22:41-42, KJV).

The poet Studdert-Kennedy's expressed it thusly:

Thy will be done. No greater words than these
Can pass from human lips, than those which rent
Their way through agony and bloody sweat
And broke the silence of Gethsemane
To save a world from sin.

16 ✑ Part of His Body

"Joined to the Immortal Head"

Its [the Lord's Prayer] very first words are Our Father. Do you now see what those words mean? They mean, quite frankly, that you are putting yourself in the place of a son of God. To put it bluntly, you are dressing up as Christ.[1]

In that way, to become holy is rather like joining a secret society. To put it at the very lowest, it must be great fun.
But you must not imagine that the new men are, in the ordinary sense, all alike. . . . Out of ourselves, into Christ, we must go. His will is to become ours and we are to think His thoughts, to "have the mind of Christ" as the Bible says.[2]

We are told in one of the creeds that the Incarnation worked "not by conversion of the Godhead into flesh, but by taking up the Manhood into God." And it seems to me that there is a real analogy between this and what I have called Transposition: that humanity, still remaining itself, is not merely counted as, but veritably drawn into, Deity.[3]

A HOLY GOD CALLS US TO BE A HOLY PEOPLE. To heed His summons, to attain that end is our final call. It is a lofty goal: attaining sanctity through sharing the very being of Christ. In the marvelous words of Peter: "According as his divine power hath given unto us all things that pertain unto life and godliness, through the knowledge of him that hath called us to glory and virtue: whereby are given unto us exceeding great and precious promises: that by these ye might be partakers of the divine nature, having escaped the corruption that is in the world through lust" (2 Pet. 1:3-4, KJV).

Lewis takes such words seriously. They're not pretty poetry or a metaphor for meditation. They're a marbled mandate, a *magna carta* of human destiny: God has made "creatures which can (if they will) be taken right out of nature, turned into 'gods.' Will they allow themselves to be taken? In a way, it is like the crisis of birth. Until we rise and follow Christ we are still parts of Nature, still in the womb of our great mother."[4]

> ## *While the obedience key opens the door to holiness, in itself obedience does not sanctify.*

We're called to rise up like recruits marshaled for battle, to join fellow pilgrims on the road to heaven. To be holy is to will God's will. This commitment enables us to be godly. Here we surrender our all so as to ultimately enjoy eternal bliss rather than strive to attain it on our own. While the obedience key opens the door to holiness, in itself obedience does not sanctify. Sanctity comes solely from God to us; it's supernaturally breathed into us by His Spirit. And it's not purely an individual thing. It comes to us, as it came to the disciples at Pentecost, as we *participate* in the body life of Christ's Body, the Church.

As a scholar, C. S. Lewis relished the solitude of study and thought, spending hours each day with books and ideas. He was not, temperamentally, a "joiner." As many of his letters make clear, much about church services and organizations bored or irritated him. He generally stressed the importance of the individual rather than social groups, which he knew easily turn demonic. His sustained criticism of various strains of "socialism" illustrated his distrust for "statism" and bureaucratic controls of any sort. There are "no ordinary people," he said. A single person, created in the image of God, is worth more than any political entity, any social organization, any reform movement.

Yet the Church is different. In a profound sense, the Church towers above all human organizations, much like a blimp above major athletic contests. She necessarily has institutional structures, but she's actually a supernatural rather than a natural organism. The Church deals with issues far more momentous than politics and economics and forever fails when she stoops to make such issues central to her endeavors. "The Church," Lewis said, "will outlive the universe; in it the individual person will outlive the universe. Everything that is joined to the immortal Head will share His immortality."[5]

When he first became a Christian, Lewis said, "I thought I could do it on my own, by retiring to my rooms and reading theology, and I wouldn't go to the Churches and Gospel Halls; and then later I found that it was the only way of flying your flag." Still more: "If there is anything in the teaching of the New Testament which is in the nature of a command, it is that you are obliged to take the Sacrament, and you can't do that without going to Church. . . . It gets you out of your solitary conceit."[6]

> ## We're called to be holy—and we are
> ## holy—together, *sharing the divine*
> ## *life of Christ within the Church.*

Thus Lewis, like John Wesley, rejected individualistic, self-centered spirituality. As he wrote: "The New Testament does not envisage solitary religion; some kind of regular assembly for worship and instruction is everywhere taken for granted in the Epistles. So must we be regular practicing members of the Church."[7] Consequently we're called, individually, to be holy, but we're also called to *join* ourselves to Christ's Body, the Church, which is declared holy by virtue of her mystical union with Him. Descriptive labels such as "Body of Christ" and "Bride of the Lamb" are not passing poetry! In his first published "Christian" work, *The Pilgrim's Regress,* Lewis credited "Mother Kirk" for rightly guiding John, the wayward pilgrim, to the saving waters of baptism, the transforming powers of Christ. Such labels for the Church are used in Scripture to indicate the organic union—the marriage—of God's Son, Christ Jesus, with His disciples. We're called to be holy—and we are holy—*together,* sharing the divine life of Christ within the Church.

In the third volume of his space trilogy, *That Hideous Strength,* one of the least attractive N.I.C.E. "scholars" is the Reverend Straik, whose "frayed clerical collar, the dark, lean, tragic face, gashed and ill-shaved and seamed, and the bitter sincerity of his manner, had struck a discordant note."[8] The Reverend Straik had a vision of bringing about a socialist utopia orchestrated by the scientists at the National Institute for Co-ordinated Experiments. That, he imagined, would be the "Kingdom of God," and he, of course, would be its high priest!

Over the years the Reverend Straik had recruited no one else to share his vision, so in the "name of Jesus" he'd simply severed himself from "all organized religion that has yet been seen in the world."[9] Taking "separatism" to its ultimate extreme, he separated himself from everyone, past and present! In his mind he stood like a solitary pine on a rocky bluff, upholding truth and righteousness, styling himself "'a poor weak, unworthy man, but the only prophet left.'"[10] (As a general rule, most of us learn to beware of strident, self-proclaimed, singular prophets!)

Unlike Straik, Lewis forever reminds his readers that the kingdom of God comes not by military violence, not even by the subtle maneuvers of human ingenuity. Neither New Age gurus nor superspiritual enthusiasts will usher it in. The Kingdom comes through down-to-earth, homey communities of faith such as the godly folks assembled around Elwin Ransom, the "Director" at St. Anne's, where the truly healthful (holy) souls wage spiritual warfare with the forces of evil represented by N.I.C.E.

Most of us understand the need for a "head" to any organism. Few of us would lose much of our personality if we lost a finger or toe. But we can't do without our head. It's the head that guides the body. When I tell my hand to "salute," it salutes! When I say to my foot "walk," it steps ahead! My heart beats, roughly 70 times a minute, because my mind signals it to do so. I breathe without conscious effort because my head orders my lungs to do their thing. My temperature remains reasonably constant, whether I'm in warm or cold weather, because my head acts like a thermostat, regulating metabolism and blood flow to make sure I remain a warm-blooded mammal.

Given that understanding, we further understand why a healthy human organization needs a "head" like Ransom, guiding the community of St. Anne's. He made it what it was. His "spirit" suffused the entire body. So, too, Jesus, the Head of His Church, guides and sustains her. Since He's holy, His workings in His body make her holy. Whatever's good and righteous in the Church, whatever's good and holy in those of us who are joined together in the Church, must be credited to her Head, Christ the Lord.

> *The primary function of the Church is to transmit the truth and to keep burning the fires of sanctity.*

We who enter God's kingdom do so through gates opened for us by a Church that preserves the truth of the gospel and makes available the manifold means of grace. The primary function of the Church is to transmit the truth and to keep burning the fires of sanctity. Thus, Lewis tells his readers, when looking for a congregation to join, "Above all you must be asking which door is the true one; not which pleases you best by its paint and paneling. In plain language, the question should never be: 'Do I like that kind of service?' but 'Are these doctrines true: Is holiness here? Does my conscience move me towards this?'"[11] The holiness of God comes alive in us as we come alive in the community of faith, as we make the truth of the Church the standard by which we live. And the transforming work of grace, sanctification, takes place as we avail ourselves of the means of grace.

Orthodox Christians in creeds confess they "believe in the Holy Church." Despite her many failures, the Church of Jesus

Christ is a necessary part of Christianity. What we mean by that, primarily, is this: Christ is the Head of the Church and His holiness permeates His body. The Church is admittedly often less than holy in her strategies and structures. And her leaders and members are often notoriously unholy! But the Church is holy because Christ is holy, and within the Church are the means whereby believers become "new men" in Christ. As Lewis says:

> **I have called Christ the "first instance" of the new man. But of course He is something much more than that. He is not merely a new man, one specimen of the species, but *the* new man. He is the origin and centre and life of all the new men. He came into the created universe, of His own will, bringing with Him the *Zoe,* the new life. . . . And He transmits it not by heredity but by what I have called "good infection." Everyone who "gets it" gets it by being "in Him."[12]**

We participate in God's sanctifying design by submitting to the work of Christ in us. We recognize, indeed revel in, our subordination to our Head. As His Body, the Church, we submit and allow Him to do His sanctifying work in us. The Church does many things, but she "exists for nothing else but to draw men into Christ, to make them little Christs."[13] So Christ's Church, Paul said, is "called to be holy" (1 Cor. 1:2). That's her aim: to share in the very likeness, the character of Christ Jesus our Lord. If you're sick, you want to get well. Health is your goal, your aim, the end of your efforts. So, too, if we're sick of our sins, we want to get well. And holiness is the goal, the aim, the end of our aspirations. Thus, in his letter to the Ephesians, Paul says: "Husbands, love your wives, just as Christ loved the church and gave himself up for her to make her holy, cleansing her by the washing with water through the word, and to present her to himself as a radiant church, without stain or wrinkle or any other blemish, but holy and blameless" (5:25-27).

To help us attain that end, Christ's Church promotes holiness, seeking to connect us to the holy One, Christ himself. She does that, in part, by calling us to separate ourselves from ungodliness. Though in the world, Jesus prayed for His disciples, who "are not of the world, even as I am not of it. Sanctify them by the truth; your word is truth" (John 17:16-17). Those who know the truth, like physicists who master the discipline and begin to grasp the intricacies of Einstein, enter into great joy in the process. And Christians, joining a Holy Church, discover the ways to become what they've ever longed to be.

Christ's Church promotes holiness, seeking to connect us to the holy One, Christ himself.

Thus we understand Paul's words in Ephesians: God "chose us in him [Jesus] before the creation of the world to be holy and blameless in his sight" (1:4). Later in the chapter, we read, "And God placed all things under his feet and appointed him to be head over everything for the church, which is his body, the fullness of him who fills everything in every way" (vv. 22-23). Christ is the *Head*. And His Church is holy as He is holy.

17 ✒ Refined by Trials

"Made Perfect Through Suffering"

*The pains
You give me are more precious
than all other gains.*[1]

IT'S NOT NECESSARILY GOD'S WILL THAT WE ALL PROSPER, though our politicians routinely get elected by promising such! Many of us wish we could, without risking failure, become millionaires by firm faith and hard work. Yet it's quite likely that what many of us want—prosperity—is not what God wants for us. In fact, He may not wish us to prosper—for Jesus said, after the rich young ruler chose not to follow Him, "How hard it is for the rich to enter the kingdom of God!" (Mark 10:23). As Lewis noted: "One of the dangers of having a lot of money is that you may be quite satisfied with the kinds of happiness money can give and so fail to realize your need for God. If everything seems to come simply by signing checks, you may forget that you are at every moment totally dependent on God."[2]

Nor is it necessarily God's will that we be well-liked. To "make friends and influence people" may be admirable, but it's apparently not God's grand plan for us. Thirty years ago a man wrote Postmaster General James Edward Day, asking that his face be placed on a postage stamp. In response, Day wrote (though he did not mail) this response: "We cannot put the face of a person on a stamp unless said person is deceased. My suggestion, therefore is that you drop dead."[3]

Of all vain things, living to please the crowd is perhaps most vain! Among the folks most quickly forgotten are the hit singers

and marquee entertainers who starred for a season. When, to-
ward the end of his life, Lewis enjoyed worldwide acclaim,
"Walter Hooper asked if he set much store by his growing fame.
Lewis answered, 'One cannot be too careful not to think of it!'"[4]
In short, our desire to be well-liked or famous, like our hanker-
ing for prosperity, easily damns us!

> *Our desire to be well-liked or*
> *famous, like our hankering for*
> *prosperity, easily damns us!*

Nor is it necessarily God's will that we all be healthy. I'd probably prosper and be well-liked if I wrote and published a slick
self-help book insisting that God wants everyone to enjoy perfect
health—that with the right techniques, or the right amount of
faith, all diseases could be eliminated. Certainly some of us get
sick and God heals us. But others of us get sick and die! In
Lewis's judgment: "Health is a great blessing, but the moment
you make health one of your main, direct objectives you start
becoming a crank and imagining there is something wrong with
you. You are only likely to get health provided you want other
things more—food, games, work, fun, open air."[5]

> *Above all else, God wants*
> *to make us holy.*

All of this is to say, as Augustine said long ago, that the great
"difference" between human beings—the difference, I might
add, that counts with God—is not found in "what ills are suffered, but what kind of man suffers them."[6] It is, you see, God's
will that we become the right kinds of persons: spiritually mature, grown up, whole persons. Above all else God wants, as the
Bible makes clear, to make us holy. He wants us to attain spiritual maturity, Christlikeness, sanctity. And whatever it takes to
sanctify us justifies the cost. Fortune hunters, diving for gold in

shipwrecked Spanish galleons, spare no expense, conserve no energy; the prize they seek seems worth any investment. So, too, with sanctity! For as Paul declared: "This is the will of God, even your sanctification" (1 Thess. 4:3, KJV).

Lewis routinely embraced the ancient understanding of suffering: wisdom, growth, maturity, holiness, develop through the tests and trials, the sufferings and pains of life. In *The Problem of Pain* he wrote: "The human spirit will not even begin to try to surrender self-will as long as all seems to be well with it."[7] At times, it seems only pain gets our attention, arousing us to the fact that something is basically wrong with the human condition. "We can rest contentedly in our sins and in our stupidities . . . . But pain insists upon being attended to. God whispers to us in our pleasures, speaks in our conscience, but shouts in our pains: it is His megaphone to rouse a deaf world."[8]

Painful truths shatter the illusions of self-sufficiency.

This megaphone is, indeed "a terrible instrument," but for some it provides "the only opportunity the bad man can have for amendment. It removes the veil; it plants the flag of truth within the fortress of a rebel soul."[9] Painful truths shatter the illusions of self-sufficiency. When sickness strikes, we're awakened to the fact that we cannot dictate life's directions, that our illusions of earthly bliss were pipe dreams. When loved ones die, we're forced to admit that our most precious bonds are as fragile as fine crystal jostled about by an earthquake. "Everyone has noticed how hard it is to turn our thoughts to God when everything is going well with us. We 'have all we want' is a terrible saying when 'all' does not include God. We find God an interruption. As St. Augustine says somewhere, 'God wants to give us something, but cannot, because our hands are full—there's nowhere for Him to put it.'"[10]

In short, though pain "is not good in itself" it may prompt us to surrender to God and His will. And this act is, in itself, good. All of us, by virtue of our membership in the human race, suffer. Once we glimpse this truth, this perspective, we can begin to understand what seems to be a consensus of biblical texts. James urges us to "consider it pure joy" when tested, for "you know that the testing of your faith develops perseverance" that makes us "mature and complete" (1:2-4). Similarly, Peter said we should, in the midst of fiery trials, "rejoice that you participate in the sufferings of Christ, so that you may be overjoyed when his glory is revealed" (1 Pet. 4:13). And Paul shared the same conviction, saying, "We also rejoice in our sufferings" (Rom. 5:3), because they develop in us a holy character rooted in the love of God (vv. 3-5). Consequently, Lewis noted, responding to an inquiry:

> **Do you know, the suffering of the innocent is less of a problem to me v. [*sic,* very] often than that of the wicked. It sounds absurd; but I've met so many innocent sufferers who seem to be gladly offering their pain to God in Christ as part of the Atonement, so patient, so meek, even so at peace, and so unselfish that we can hardly doubt they are being, as St. Paul says, "made perfect by suffering." On the other hand I meet selfish egoists in whom suffering seems to produce only resentment, hate, blasphemy, and more egoism. They are the real problem.**[11]

Lewis discovered, as will most of us, that there's a basic life principle that insists, as some tough-talking coaches say: no pain, no gain! Late in life Lewis married, and after his wife, Joy, died of cancer, anonymously published as a diary *A Grief Observed.* Here he noted: "What do people mean when they say 'I am not afraid of God because I know He is good?' Have they never even been to a dentist?"[12] Employing another medical metaphor, he noted that God is much more like a surgeon than a counselor: "The more we believe that God hurts only to heal, the less we can believe that there is any use in begging for tenderness. A cruel man might be bribed—might grow tired of his vile sport—might have a temporary fit of mercy, as alcoholics have fits of sobriety. But suppose that what you are up against is a surgeon whose intentions are wholly good. The kinder and more conscientious he is, the more inexorably he will go on cutting."[13]

We might beg for relief, cry out in anger, telling him that if he really loved us he'd stop inflicting pain, but a good surgeon wouldn't spare us. For "if he yielded to your entreaties, if he stopped before the operation was complete, all the pain up to that point would have been useless. But is it credible that such extremities of torture should be necessary for us? Well, take your choice. The tortures occur. If they are unnecessary, then there is no God or a bad one. If there is a good God, then these tortures are necessary. For no even moderately good Being could possibly inflict or permit them if they weren't."[14]

In one of his letters, Lewis insisted we must not interpret suffering as punishment sent directly from God simply to pain us: "I believe that all pain is contrary to God's will, absolutely but not relatively. When I am taking a thorn out of my own finger (or a child's finger) the pain is 'absolutely' contrary to my will. . . . But I *do* will what caused the pain, relatively to the given situation; i.e. granted the thorn I prefer the pain to leaving the thorn where it is."[15] Shifting the analogy, he further explains: "A mother spanking a child would be in the same position; she would rather cause it this pain than let it go on pulling the cat's tail, but we would like it better if no situation which demands a smack had arisen."[16]

Lewis's truth is amplified in the works of Bernie Siegel, who teaches at Yale University Medical School, and has dealt with terminally ill cancer patients for many years. Those who quickly succumb to the disease usually complain about their fate, whining "why me, Lord." Those who live longer, some who against all odds recover, usually say "try me, Lord." To take life's difficulties as tests, to see in our various pains some possibility for growth and character development, opens our minds to a great biblical truth.

Lewis was one of the great Christian scholars of his day. Most of his life he taught at Oxford University. Early in his career, shortly after his conversion, he published a book, *The Pilgrim's Regress,* with some allusions he later regretted. The book angered some of Oxford's powerful professors, as did Lewis's subsequent success as a Christian writer and his vigorous witness to his Christian faith. Subsequently his colleagues refused to promote him to the position of a professor. He remained a tutor, the bottom rung of the academic ladder, throughout his career there—though he was, witnesses affirm, Oxford's most renowned and esteemed teacher.

Difficult though it was, Lewis had to regularly tutor students and received less money than an established professor. He never had a secretary and had to answer his own mail. How unfair! Yet Lewis later confessed that such difficulties did in fact greatly aid him, both as a scholar and as a Christian. He stayed in touch with his world through his students and correspondents. He refused to let his colleagues' envy sour him or deflect him from scholarly and popular writing. He simply accepted the weights placed upon him to develop his moral muscle. He was a better man as a result. And it was as a better man he influenced his world.

> *God allows all of us to die, so apparently our longevity is not the central melody of God's symphony for planet earth.*

One of the greatest "evils," of course, is death. As Lewis saw it, however, death may not in fact be all that evil. Given our predicament as fallen creatures, needing eternal life, death as a doorway to such bliss is ultimately a great blessing. "Human Death is a result of sin and the triumph of Satan. But it is also the means of redemption from sin, God's medicine for Man and His weapon against Satan."[17] In fact, God allows all of us to die, so apparently our longevity is not the central melody of God's symphony for planet earth. Death, in fact, "is a safety-device because once Man has fallen, natural immortality would be the one utterly hopeless destiny for him."[18]

One of the winsome characteristics of the strangely shaped but unfallen creatures on the planet Malacandra, recorded in *Out of the Silent Planet,* is their lack of fear of death. Thus they rejoiced in the life given them and fearlessly faced death when duty called. Toward the end of the story, responding to a threat

from Weston, Oyarsa, the planet's ruler, said: "The weakest of
my people does not fear death. It is the Bent One, the lord of
your world, who wastes your lives and befouls them with flying
from what you know will overtake you in the end. If you were
subjects of Maleldil you would have peace."[19]

Similarly, in *Miracles* Lewis notes:

> **On the one hand Death is the triumph of Satan,
> the punishment of the Fall, and the last enemy. . . .
> On the other hand, only he who loses his life will save
> it. We are baptized into the death of Christ, and it is
> the remedy for the Fall. Death is, in fact, what some
> modern people call "ambivalent." It is Satan's great
> weapon and also God's great weapon: it is holy and
> unholy; our supreme disgrace and our only hope; the
> thing Christ came to conquer and the means by which
> He conquered.[20]**

Facing death, most of us feel faint. No human helpers can
fully help us in the presence of our last enemy. But there's One
who faced, experienced, and triumphed over death. Jesus came
to terms with death in Gethsemane and died on Calvary, utterly
surrendered to God's will. Thus the ultimate suffering, death, is
the final doorway to bliss. "Christ shed tears at the grave of
Lazarus and sweated blood in Gethsemane: the Life of Lives
that was in Him detested this penal obscenity not less than we
do, but more."[21] So Jesus told Martha, when Lazarus died: "Thy
brother shall rise again. Martha saith unto him, I know that he
shall rise again in the resurrection at the last day. Jesus said unto her, I am the resurrection, and the life: he that believeth in
me, though he were dead, yet shall he live: and whosoever
liveth and believeth in me shall never die" (John 11:23-26, KJV).

⧁ **PART FIVE** ⧁

HOLY, HOLY, HOLY GOD

18 ✍ Holy Father

"God Himself Has Taught Us How to Speak of Him"

If "religion" means simply what man says about God, and not what God does about man, then Pantheism almost is religion. And "religion" in that sense has, in the long run, only one really formidable opponent—namely Christianity.[1]

A FATHER CAME HOME TO HIS FIVE KIDS and tantalized them with a toy he'd purchased. He promised to give it to the one "who is the most obedient, never talks back to Mother and does everything she says." The youngsters paused for a momentary huddle, then in unison said: "You do, Daddy. So you get to play with the toy." So much for the image of dictatorial dads! The story, to a degree, subtly reveals today's loss of fatherly authority. In fact one of the great problems in America today is fatherlessness! In a disturbing study, *Fatherless America,* David Blankenhorn asserts the lack of fathers "is the leading cause of declining child well-being in our society."[2] Consequently, we've lost societal health, for "a good society celebrates the ideal of a man who puts his family first."[3]

There is, more deeply, a bond between a good society and a Father God who protects and provides for His children. The Church of Jesus Christ ever acknowledges the importance of Jesus' Father. To pray the Lord's prayer we begin: "Our Father which art in heaven" (Matt. 6:9, KJV). Yet this ancient invocation has, amazingly, become offensive to some in our society. It has become so offensive in fact that some are trying to revise it! A recent *Newsweek* article reports that "in the nation's elite divinity schools, students are taught . . . [that] God the Father is out, unless coupled with God the Mother. 'She Who Is,' is Elizabeth Johnson's preferred phrase; others talk simply of 'Godself' . . . Few theologians these days seem to want a God who takes charge, assumes responsibility, fights for his children, makes demands, risks rebuffs, punishes as well as forgives. In a word, a father."[4]

> *Idolatry*—watering down *or diluting the truth about God—has circled like a stalled hurricane over the coastlines of history.*

Yet what we call God clearly matters. For we understand Him, we approach Him, through the words we use to describe Him. Throughout the past, idolatry—*watering-down* or *diluting* the truth about God—has circled like a stalled hurricane over the coastlines of history. Idolatry sets up rivals to revelation. Idolatry reveres creatures rather than the Creator, crafting household or tribal deities more manageable and understandable to man, piecing together intellectual theories or sensual rituals more satisfying to us. Idolatry is arguably the great flaw of our species. Refusing to worship the one true God, we paste together self-help manuals and fall to our knees before hosts of in-our-image images.

Idolatry flows, like a serpentine mountain stream, from a remote reservoir: pantheism. If all is God and God is all—if everything is somehow God—then everything we turn to, whatever we make, is part of a divine realm. In Lewis's judgment, "Pantheism certainly is (as its advocates would say) congenial to the modern mind; but the fact that a shoe slips on easily does not prove that it is a new shoe—much less that it will keep your feet dry. Pantheism is congenial to our minds not because it is the final stage of a slow process of enlightenment, but because it is almost as old as we are."[5]

Pantheism may be the "most primitive of all religions,"

Lewis suggested. "It is immemorial in India," and only in Plato and Aristotle did the Greeks transcend it. "Modern Europe escaped it only while she remained predominantly Christian," but philosophers such as Giordano Bruno, Baruch Spinoza, and Hegel resurrected it. "Pantheism is in fact the permanent natural bent of the human mind; the permanent level below which man sometimes sinks, . . . but above which his own unaided efforts can never raise him for very long."[6] "Men are reluctant to pass over from the notion of an abstract and negative deity to the living God. I do not wonder. Here lies the deepest tap-root of Pantheism and of the objection to traditional imagery. It was hatred not, at bottom, because it pictured Him as man but because it pictured Him as king, or even as warrior. The Pantheists' God does nothing, demands nothing. He is there, if you wish for Him, like a book on a shelf. He will not pursue you."[7]

We're endlessly inclined to slide into such comfortable concepts of God! So it's critical to carefully cling to the ever-ancient, ever-new truth Scripture reveals to us concerning God. We mustn't first envision things we like—buffaloes or butterflies, kindly uncles or tender mothers—and then imagine that God resembles whatever warms our hearts. Here Lewis reminds us of the *objective* pole of truth, that truthfulness is shaped by the Truth, the very being of God. Thus good theology, like a good topographical map, reveals what is inflexible. "Theology," Lewis wrote, "means 'the science of God,' and I think any man who wants to think about God at all would like to have the clearest and most accurate ideas above Him which are available."[8]

This means we need to understand, so far as we're able, the nature of God. A highly regarded Anglican theologian, contemporary with Lewis, Eric Mascall, insisted that the Trinity is more than a doctrine: "the Trinity is God," which means "there are three divine Persons eternally united in one life of complete perfection and beatitude." This is not sheer speculative theology! "It is the secret of God's most intimate life and being, into which, in his infinite love and generosity, he has admitted us; and is therefore to be accepted with amazed and exultant gratitude."[9]

Lewis concurred: "When you come to knowing God," he insisted, "the initiative lies on His side."[10] Since God consistently, and in the New Testament forcefully, revealed himself as our *Fa-*

ther—the Maker of heaven and earth, the first of three Persons in the blessed Trinity—no other name rightly portrays Him. Substituting names that we prefer—"Grandfather" or "Life-force" or "Mother"—leaves us with less than a holy God. Naming God is no trivial issue, as the third commandment makes clear, for basic to biblical faith is the conviction that names reveal essences.

One of America's finest Evangelical theologians, Donald Bloesch, insists: "When we speak of God as Father in the biblical sense, it should be borne in mind that this is not a mere symbol."[11] The Church's greatest theologians—Augustine, Aquinas, Barth—all agree "that when Father refers to God, especially in the context of devotion, the word is not figurative, but closer to being literal in that it is practically transparent to what it signifies. The same can be said about Jesus Christ when he is called Son and Lord."[12]

Addressing this issue, Augustine wrote: "It is one thing when you are taught to honor God in that He is God; but another thing when thou art taught to honor Him in that He is Father."[13] Many, he noted, looking around the pagan world, revere a "Creator." Many religions in the ancient world celebrated spiritual beings of various kinds. But only Christians are "taught to honor Him in that He is Father" of our Lord and Savior Jesus Christ.[14]

Lewis, with both historical perspective and prophetic insight, glimpsed what would happen should we seek to depart from Augustine's position and alter our image of God—imagining, as some do, that theologically we can flip a coin to decide whether to refer to God as Mother or as both Mother and Father. Some imagine that since God's not a sexual being (as everyone agrees) we're free to revision Him as "Her" if we so desire. He sensed the currents of cultural winds blowing theological gliders in directions demonstrably evident only after his death. Thus, considering some early advocates of feminine terms for God, he wondered: "Suppose a man says that we might just as well pray to 'Our Mother which art in heaven' as to 'Our Father.' Suppose he suggests that the Incarnation might just as well have taken a female as a male form, and the Second Person of the Trinity may as well be called the Daughter as the Son. Suppose, finally, that the mystical marriage were reversed, that the Church were the Bridegroom and Christ the Bride."[15]

All such "supposes" have in fact come to pass in the decades following Lewis's death. Influential neognostic "feminists," bureaucratically imposed "inclusive language" hymns and creeds, have dictatorially sought to reshape the vocabulary of the Christian world. Much more than vocabulary stands at risk. What's really at stake is the Christian truth about who God is. As Bloesch asserts: "The debate in the church today is not primarily over women's rights but over the doctrine of God." There's a great struggle between those who "believe in a God who acts in history" and those who believe in a "God who simply resides within nature," between those who "believe in a God who created the world out of nothing" and those who believe "in a God whose infinite fecundity gave rise to a world that is inseparable from his own being?"[16]

> *"But Christians think that*
> *God Himself has taught us*
> *how to speak of Him."*

Half a century ago, Lewis predicted that many "Christian feminist" proposals, if implemented, would install an entirely "different religion." Certainly most non-Christian religions have featured goddesses, served by priestesses of various sorts. "But they are religions quite different in character from Christianity." Many today wonder "why not?" call God "Mother" if it makes them feel better?[17] After all, "since God is in fact not a biological being and has no sex, what can it matter whether we say He or She, Father or Mother, Son or Daughter? But Christians think that God Himself has taught us how to speak of Him. To say that it does not matter is to say either that all the masculine imagery is not inspired, is merely human in origin, or else that, though inspired, is quite arbitrary and unessential."[18]

Christians call God "Father" simply because Jesus did. In the Old Testament, God is rarely addressed as "Father"—only 15 references, of which only 2 use the word in prayer. In the New Testament, however, the word "Father" is used 245 times. Jesus himself used it 170 times! And virtually every New Testament use of "Father" is in prayer—praying Jesus' way! It's clear that Christians pray because Jesus is God's Son and it is by virtue of His work in us that we are free to call God "Father."

We come to God in prayer, saying "Our Father," because Jesus said to. In this area I cheerfully follow the bumper sticker that says, "God said it. I believe it. That settles it." In some areas it may not be too clear what God said. But when I pray *to* the Father *through* the Son *in* the Holy Spirit, I know precisely the word to use: Father. God's Son said it. I believe it. That settles it! If Jesus had said we're to call God the "Great Pumpkin," as a Christian I'd do it—or else admit I no longer follow Him.

My wife is a travel agent, an independent businesslady. I know she knows the business! One day I was presumptuously trying to advise her on a trip she'd planned. The advice stopped when she coolly looked at me and said: "I'm the travel agent!" End of discussion! If she tells me something about an airline ticket, I believe her. It would be truly stupid for me to take a ticket she's processed and emend it—trying to change a reservation from Denver to Seattle! She knows what she does. And Jesus, God's Son, knows how to pray to God! If He says pray "Our Father," that's good enough for me. As C. S. Lewis says: "Christians think that God Himself has taught us how to speak of Him."

We live and move and have our being in realities that inform *words*. Misguided words, like ricocheting bullets, fail to rightly correspond with reality. So word disputes involve much more than personal preferences—they revolve around more or less accurate concepts of reality. Today's scholars who insert a feminine contour into our understanding of God defiantly jettison the traditional trinitarianism of the Church, often claiming no more justification than the fact that her "androcentric" language and "patriarchal" structures offend them. Some even approve efforts to synthesize Yahweh with Astarte, blasphemously adding a "Canaanite fertility goddess in the present-day image of God."[19]

Though long dead by the time such thinkers exerted much influence in Christian circles, C. S Lewis—unlike many "modernists" of his day who daily blew with the wind—upheld the ancient views of classical Christian theology. This included the traditional understanding of both sexual and gender differences and their relevance to biblical imagery for God. In some of his fictional work, especially the third volume of his space trilogy, *That Hideous Strength,* he makes it clear that men and women should revere the Creator's design for the sexes. The book's main theme is launched with its first sentence, taken from the *Book of Common Prayer:* "Matrimony was ordained, thirdly, for the mutual society, help, and comfort that the one ought to have of the other."[20] As men and women accept their roles, obeying God's rules for them as life partners, they find joy and peace in a right understanding of and relationship with their Lord.

Having indicated the basic reason we call God "Father," let's try and understand why it makes sense. It has nothing to do with the superiority of males, nor with any projection of male characteristics on God. Perhaps you've heard about the little girl who wondered why there are more women than men. An aspiring biblical scholar, she reasoned, "Well, first God made Adam, and He wasn't too pleased with the result. So He made Eve. And He was so pleased with her that He's been making more women than men ever since!"

We call God "Father" not because He's male! One radical feminist scholar, Mary Daly, insists that "if God is male, then male is God." But she refuses to admit that Christians have never had a human "male" in mind when calling God "Father." In fact, all mature believers know God is wholly God, and He is not a human being, much less a male! Yet it is clear that we better understand God as a "person" than an animal or a vegetable! We call God "Father" because, in language, the masculine "gender" better enables us to understand Him. Unfortunately, we've failed to uphold the distinction between "sex" and "gender." Sex refers to biology—male and female. Gender refers to masculine, feminine, and neuter *words* that apply to many things quite independent of sex. This is because, as Lewis explained in a fascinating passage in *Perelandra,* the second volume of his space trilogy, "gender" underlies all creation. Concluding the story—where the "Green Lady," the queen, has resisted Satan's temptation and been joined to the king, doing what Adam and Eve failed to accomplish on earth, Ransom glimpsed "the real meaning of gender." Philologists like Ransom know that virtually all languages identify inanimate objects as masculine or feminine. Clearly "gender" is not "an imaginative extension of sex. Our ancestors did not make mountains masculine because they projected male characteristics into them. The real process is the reverse. Gender is a reality, and a more fundamental reality than sex. Sex is, in fact, merely the adaptation to organic life of a fundamental polarity which divides all created beings."[21] Females are feminine and males are masculine, yet our language reveals how "Masculine and Feminine meet us on planes of reality where male and female would be simply meaningless. Masculine is not attenuated male, nor feminine attenuated female. On the contrary, the male and females of organic creatures are rather faint and blurred reflections of masculine and feminine."[22]

> ### *We use the word "Father" as His proper name, the only name Jesus gave us with which to pray.*

More than understanding gender, we must understand the *vocative voice*. We use the vocative voice when we address someone. When I say "Jim," I address a certain man I know. When I say "Dad" to my father, I address Him as a unique person, the only "dad" I have. When I call my father "Dad," it's like calling Jim "Jim." In the vocative voice, it becomes a proper name. So, addressing God, we use the word "Father" as His proper name, the only name Jesus gave us with which to pray.

Still more, "Father" is a unique analogy, not a mere metaphor or sign. We continually use metaphors to explain things. Metaphors operate on a horizontal plane, enabling us to compare things. In the Bible, metaphors abound regarding God. He's compared to a rock. A solid rock! We could add—a rock as solid as Gibraltar! Such metaphors give us some ideas concerning the nature of God. But we don't pray "Dear Rock." As Lewis explained; "Grammatically the things we say of Him are 'metaphorical': but in a deeper sense it is our physical and psychic energies that are mere 'metaphors' of the real Life which is God. Divine Sonship is, so to speak, the solid of which biological sonship is merely a diagrammatic representation on the flat."[23]

Such analogies—figures of speech correlating divine and human worlds—partake of what they refer to and refer us to realities above us, too mysterious for scientific definition. Thus the Cross portrays Christ's work for us on Calvary. It's a wooden cross, yes, but it stands for much more than a simple example of a man who died. The Cross contains meanings too marvelous for words. It's an analogy. Were I to place an icon depicting Christ's crucifixion on the entryway of a church, alongside a recent picture of me, most everyone would choose to step on my visage rather than Christ's. The word "Father" is an analogy, not a metaphor. To call God "Father" means more than attributing to Him some of the characteristics of our earthly fathers. As an analogy, "Father" represents the transcendent Source of life, the One who spoke the cosmos into being.

Collapsing the wall that separates the sexes runs counter to the creative will of God, so evident in the deeper masculine/feminine polarities of the universe. Thus we rightly call the sun "Father" and the earth "Mother." As Lewis noted: "The marriage relation between Father Sky (or Dyaus) and Mother Earth forces itself on the imagination. He is on top, she lies under him. He does things to her (shines and, more important, rains upon her, into her): out of her, in response, come forth crops—just as calves come out of cows or babies out of wives. In a word, he begets, she bears."[24]

More's at stake in gender language than treating men and women equitably—something all Christians are called to do. What's at stake is the basic attitude we take regarding creation and the Creator. As Bloesch says: "To switch from the masculine to the feminine in our descriptions of God in a service of worship is inevitably to present a false picture of God—a deity who is bisexual or androgynous rather than one who transcends the polarity of the sexes." Equally wrongheaded are efforts "to think of God as an impersonal or suprapersonal ground of being, as do Christian Scientists who generally address God as Mother-Father."[25] Most deeply at stake is the difference between theism and pantheism, a difference Lewis insisted is as old as human history. Whenever folks substitute "Mother" for "Father," pantheism slips like rain through the seams of a saturated tent, for a "goddess" creator squeezes creation out of herself, like toothpaste from a tube, exuding her own body into the world.

When we call God "Father" we avoid the pantheism that seems to accompany virtually all non-Judeo-Christian forms of religion. Unless God stands outside creation, as a father remains separate from the child he helps conceive, He becomes simply a part of the process of creation. Calling God "Mother" inexorably leads to a Goddess worship that forever embraces pantheism—simply because a mother conceives a child inside herself and the child is part of her.

What happens is evident in *The New Century Hymnal,* recently endorsed by the United Church of Christ. According to a report in *Christianity Today,* "God is only rarely depicted as Father, Lord, and Ruler and never as King and Master. Among the new designations for God are the "All-inclusive One," "Great Spirit," "Architect Divine," "Womb of Life," and "Source of Being." More personal appellations include "Mother," "Partner," and "Friend." Such labels, Lewis recognized, are ancient pantheistic metaphors. They're attractive to us, he explained, because: "An 'impersonal God'—well and good. A subjective God of beauty, truth and goodness, inside our own heads—better still. A formless life-force surging through us, a vast power which we can tap—best of all. But God himself, alive, pulling at the other end of the cord, perhaps approaching us at an infinite speed, the hunter, king, husband—that is quite another matter."[26]

Further illustrating such tendencies in contemporary "Christian" circles: "The doxology is no longer 'Praise Father, Son and Holy Ghost,' but rather 'One God, Triune, whom we adore.'" The new version of the Gloria Patri ("Glory Be to the Father") is "Glory to the Creator." Finally: "In the revised Apostles' Creed, Jesus is referred to as 'God's only Child' rather than 'God's only Son.'" The first sentence of the creed is now rendered "I believe in God the Father-Mother almighty, creator of heaven and earth." The last section of the revised Nicene Creed becomes, "We believe in the Holy Spirit, the Sovereign, the giver of life, who proceeds from the Father-Mother, and from the Child."[27]

Such examples must give us pause: in such language the Christian Church faces an assault on the deepest level of her faith. No wonder a United Church of Christ theologian declares that the new hymnal marks the "advent of a new religion." The

Trinity, the Incarnation, the fundamentals of our tradition, now stand rejected. For more than a century, "liberals" of various types have worked to undermine the historic faith. We face, in our day, a crisis that is as momentous as that faced by Christians in the fourth century. The question is: how will we respond?

Several years ago Chuck Colson was asked to address a large Evangelical gathering. Then he received a letter warning him not to use certain words and to emend any version of the Bible whose wording violated the speech code. In response, Colson drafted a new speech and gave an impassioned message calling the group to affirm "the inerrant Word of God and the need to guard orthodoxy." And that's what we do when we incessantly pray, Jesus' way: *"Our Father,"* never relenting when facing those who would have us alter our words in approaching God.

19 ✍ Holy Son

"The 'Good and Terrible' Lion of Judah"

"Is he a man?" asked Lucy.
"Aslan a man!" said Mr. Beaver sternly. "Certainly
not. I tell you he is the King of the wood and the
son of the great Emperor-Beyond-the-Sea. Don't
you know who is the King of Beasts? Aslan is a
lion—the Lion, the great Lion."
"Ooh!" said Susan, "I'd thought he was a man.
Is he—quite safe? . . .
"Safe?" said Mr. Beaver. "Don't you hear what
Mrs. Beaver tells you? Who said anything about
safe? 'Course he isn't safe. But he's good.
He's the King, I tell you."[1]

THE AWE WE FEEL IN THE PRESENCE OF A HOLY GOD rightly extends to His equally holy Son, Jesus Christ. Our knowledge of a "holy God" gets its bearings, like a compass pointing northward, from Christ Jesus. Yet how rarely do we moderns seem *awed* by Him! How rarely does the word "holy" leap into our minds when we think of "Jesus." Instead we're tempted to think He's just like us, though a bit kinder. He's a nice guy, a good friend who's always around to hang out with or help us when we need it. He's mainly come to just "be there" for us! So we're routinely urged to snuggle up and find comfort in the protective arms of a Jesus who's markedly less than *Yahweh* enfleshed.

The 20th century's "therapeutic society" has secured the virtual triumph of what C. S. Lewis called "Christianity-and-water, the view which simply says there is a good God in Heaven and everything is all right—leaving out all the difficult and terrible doctrines about sin and hell and the devil, and the redemption."[2] Such views reduce Jesus to a "man-for-others," a compassionate friend, ignoring the soaring affirmations of the Scriptures concerning His deity.

As a layman, C. S. Lewis tried to distance himself from most of the theological wars that have so divided the Church across the centuries. Many issues were not worth fighting for. Yet he boldly declared his distaste for any alleged "Christianity" that diluted the strong dogmas set forth in the Scriptures and classic creeds of the Early Church. He deeply lamented the triumph of the theological "liberalism" that John Henry Newman had so prophetically decried a century before, detecting therein a mood utterly adverse to authentic Christianity. (Some of the same tendencies in 18th-century Deism helped inspire the Wesleyan revival in England.)

Thus Lewis shared some of Newman's and Wesley's convictions. Shortly before he become a cardinal, Newman said he had all his life "resisted to the best of my powers the spirit of Liberalism in religion." Such Liberalism decreed "that there is no positive truth in religion, but that one creed is as good as another," refusing to recognize "any religion as true. It teaches that all are to be tolerated, for all are matters of opinion."[3]

> *Generally speaking, theological liberals portray Jesus as a good-natured, mild-mannered, inoffensive champion of philanthropy and peace, social justice and tolerance.*

Toward the end of his life, Lewis noted that "Liberal Christians" felt threatened by orthodox believers such as himself:

"They themselves find it impossible to accept most of the articles of the 'faith once given to the saints.' They are nevertheless extremely anxious that some vestigial religion which they (not we) can describe as 'Christianity' should continue to exist and make numerous converts. They think these converts will come in only if this religion is sufficiently 'demythologized.' That the ship must be lightened if she is to keep afloat."[4]

Generally speaking, theological liberals portray Jesus as a good-natured, mild-mannered, inoffensive champion of philanthropy and peace, social justice and tolerance. Above all, they insist, Christ was compassionate and kind, rather like a maiden aunt anxious to ingratiate herself with nieces and nephews, sweetly accepting us, passively overlooking whatever we may be doing. In the memorable words of H. Richard Niebuhr, liberals thought "a God without wrath brought men without sin into a kingdom without judgment through the ministrations of a Christ without a Cross."[5]

Largely absent from much modern preaching is the awesome King, the Lord Christ, who eternally reigns and will come again not as a little babe in Bethlehem but as a conquering warrior. The tawny, sinuous Lord who is like Aslan, the powerful lion in Lewis's *The Chronicles of Narnia*! To see Jesus thusly—in His fullness, His holiness—collapses our knees in submission. As the children venturing in Narnia discover, "People who have not been in Narnia sometimes think that a thing cannot be good and terrible at the same time."[6]

But that's precisely what Jesus is. He's "more than a carpenter." He's also more than a Jewish peasant aligned with Marx's working classes—the Jesus of faddish "liberation theology." He's more than a wise man, giving shrewd advice on life—the Jesus of university lecture halls. He's more than a healer, pouring ointment on sore bodies and souls—the Jesus of TV faith-healers. He's more than a reformer, calling us to establish economic equity and end discrimination—the Jesus of social justice crusaders. He's more than a "man for others" who willingly sacrificed himself in a dramatic demonstration of brotherly love —the Jesus of many Sunday morning homilies urging us to simply ask "What Would Jesus Do?" in daily decisions.

While it's true that Christ, the Word who "was with God"

and "was God" (John 1:1), emptied himself of some aspects of deity when He assumed human nature (as Paul makes clear in Phil. 2:1-11), it's equally true that the resurrected Christ will return in glory, as a mighty roaring lion. As Augustine said: "For He was not made man in such manner that He lost His being as God. Man was added to Him, God not lost to Him."[7] We are, says Thomas Aquinas, "given to understand that He came down from Heaven by assuming an earthly nature, yet in such way that He continues to remain in Heaven." Ascending into heaven, He now sits at the Father's right hand. We're told this, Aquinas continues, so we can "understand that the Son is seated with the Father as being in no way inferior to Him according to the divine nature, but on a par with Him in all things."[8] Accordingly, in Lewis's *The Lion, the Witch, and the Wardrobe,* Mrs. Beaver told the children, "Of course he [Aslan] isn't safe. But he's good. He's the King, I tell you."[9]

This is just as John envisions in the Book of Revelation, where "one of the elders saith unto me, Weep not: behold, the Lion of the tribe of Judah, the Root of David, hath prevailed to open the book, and to loose the seven seals thereof" (5:5, KJV). At the opening of the seals, "every creature which is in heaven, and on the earth, and under the earth, and such as are in the sea, and all that are in them, heard I saying, Blessing, and honour, and glory, and power, be unto him that sitteth upon the throne, and unto the Lamb for ever and ever" (v. 13, KJV).

> *Our very being finds itself drawn,*
> *as if by the power of gravity,*
> *to holy persons.*

Just hearing such biblical passages read elicits in some of us that deeply alluring "rumor of angels" that forever haunts the deeper caves of human experience. This awe is awakened, as if by the sun's rays streaming through the window at dawn, by the holy One. For just as we physically have the capacity to awaken and arise, so, too, our minds are naturally attuned to aspects of the holy in our world. And when we see such, as when we see the Milky Way in all its splendor for the first time, we're entranced.

Our very being finds itself drawn, as if by the power of gravity, to holy persons. Thus we witnessed, during the final years of her life, an unceasing parade of pilgrims to Calcutta, India, where people simply hoped to see and perhaps meet Mother Teresa. Her words were words of wisdom, but her life was what mattered. She was a "holy" woman! Similarly, we may well come to admire the wisdom of Jesus, following the instructions of the best of all rabbis, but it is only awe at His sanctity that prompts us to kneel, enraptured at the numinous splendor of the Christ.

One of Lewis's Narnian stories, *Prince Caspian,* describes Narnia following its conquest by Telmarine barbarians, who have virtually destroyed the "Old Narnians," the talking animals and creatures resident in the original creation. The earthly adventurers, the Pevensie children, discover a ruined castle, Cair Paravel, then venture forth to battle alongside Aslan, who has just arrived to expel the evil occupying forces. "At the sight of Aslan the cheeks of the Telmarine soldiers became the colour of cold gravy, their knees knocked together, and many fell on their faces. They had not believed in lions and this made their fear greater. Even the Red Dwarfs, who knew that he came as a friend, stood with open mouths and could not speak."[10]

At the Cross we see ourselves as we really are.

The "Talking Beasts" felt comfortable in Aslan's presence and milled around him. The children, however, including the soon-to-be-crowned King Caspian of Narnia, knelt before him, awaiting orders. In a concluding ceremony, Aslan placed himself in a glade, and his followers came before him, dressed in their finest wardrobes. Adorned with silk and gold, jewels and feathers, "they were almost too bright to look at." "Yet nobody's eyes were on them or the children. The living and strokable gold of Aslan's mane outshone them all."[11] Then he spoke. "'Peace,' said Aslan in the low voice which was nearest to his growl. The earth seemed to shake a little and every living thing in the grove became still as stone."[12]

Similarly, if ever we see Him, we grow still and kneel before the Christ of Golgotha. Here, above all, we sense what Rudolph Otto called *mysterium tremendum et fascinosum*. To see justice and mercy joined in the dying Son of God, to feel the love flowing from hands and feet, moves us into the mysterious realm of blood sacrifice and vicarious redemption—truths that grip us as in a vice while slipping away from our tidy compartments of logic and chalkboard diagrams. At the Cross we see ourselves as we really are. And we find nothing matters more than contrition, confession, repentance, obedience. In the Crucified One we see, as Isaiah saw, that God is holy, holy, holy. On the Cross we know it took Someone utterly better than we, absolutely holy, whose remedy alone suffices for our sin.

Yet our awe at Jesus' deity, His holy otherness, must not decrease our joy at His humanity, His one-with-us-ness. He is fully God and fully man! In Augustine's words, He is the "saint of saints." To Lewis, he is "the Only True Man" who ever lived. Comparing our lost estate as humans to a debilitating illness, Lewis explained:

> **Medicine labours to restore "natural" structure or "normal" function. But greed, egoism, self-deception and self-pity are not unnatural or abnormal in the same sense as astigmatism or a floating kidney. For who, in Heaven's name, would describe as natural or was not at all like the psychologist's picture of the integrated, balanced, adjusted, happily married, employed, popular citizen. You can't really be very well "adjusted" to your world if it says you "have a devil" and ends by nailing you up naked to a stake of wood.[13]**

No questions more recurrently haunt man's history than these: "What is man?" "Who am I?" "What ought I be?" "What is the nature of human nature?" Classical education, rooted in Greek thought, focused on such questions. Educators endeavored to facilitate self-discovery, self-development, largely ignoring the "practical" knowledge and skills needed to make it in the marketplace. Paul also reflected upon such questions by contrasting the polarities between the first man, Adam, and the second Man, Jesus Christ. Before his fall in the Garden of Eden, Adam possessed all the fully human attributes assigned him by the Creator. He was fully human. He was, in fact, the "natural man."

In Lewis's *The Pilgrim's Regress,* we read "Mother Kirk's Story," an account of our first parents' fall from grace. As she explained, the Landlord chose to give a beautiful farm to a young married man. "For you must know that he drew up a very different lease from the kind you have nowadays. It was a lease in perpetuity on his side, for he promised never to turn them out; but on their side, they could leave when they chose, as long as one of their sons was there, to take the farm on, and then go up to live with him in the mountains."[14] The Landlord forbade them to eat a mountain-apple, which was not good for them, but otherwise they were markedly free and enjoyed a marvelous existence. However, the young couple listened to a rebellious child of the Landlord and ate an apple. As Mother Kirk recounted: "And at the moment he put out his hand and plucked the fruit there was an earthquake, and the country cracked open all the way across from North to South; and ever since, instead of the farm, there has been this gorge, which the country people call the grand Canyon. But in my language its name is *Peccatum Adae.*"[15] Adam's sin—*Peccatum Adae*—that's our flaw!

What was lost and can now be regained, is holiness.

Some of that original goodness slipped away as Adam and Eve turned from Light to Darkness, sliding into the silted quicksand of sin. Thereby Adam and Eve lost some of their humanness, became as Lewis said, "half men," whereas the Lord Jesus alone, since Adam's fall, was "the only true Man."[16] Jesus, the second Adam, restored our race, released us from the penalty of sin, by paving the way for us to regain what was lost in Eden. What was lost and can now be regained, is holiness.

Attaining holiness, our true potential, hardly suits the spirit of any age—especially ours! Many talk glibly about "personal development," "attaining one's potential," and "developing healthy self-esteem." In part, that's because we tend to slide on the surface of things, skating on the thin ice of a lake that is warming to spring. Noting this tendency, in his book, *Take and Read,* Eugene Peterson says:

> Herman Melville once wrote to a friend, "I love all men who dive." Most of us do. But where do we find them? Not in the men and women who attract attention. The trivial and evil feed the appetite for gossip in a journalistic culture. Neither goodness nor righteousness make headlines. Anything that cannot be programmed for mass production, particularly moral excellence, is discarded. Maturity, since it cannot be mastered in a semester course, is no longer a personal goal.[17]

Jesus, however, shows us what cannot be mastered in a semester, much less distilled from the pages of the latest self-help best-seller. He calls us to follow Him, in a lifetime of discipline. This makes us mature, enabling us to realize our potential as men and women created in God's image. Jesus teaches us well because He lived well—he lived life as it should be lived. He was, as Augustine suggested, the "Saint of saints."[18]

Thus the call to live as Jesus lived, to be holy, is a radical call! In *The Pilgrim's Regress,* Lewis's alter ego, John, meets "Mr. Sensible," who urges him to sit back and enjoy the pleasures of self-indulgence, what he called "Urbanity." Questioned concerning issues of ultimate concern, Mr. Sensible responded: "The proper study of mankind is man, and I have always left useless speculations alone."[19] He claimed that his view, *Le bon sens,* was shared by Aristotle, who urged us to settle for the "golden mean." Compromise, finding the way of least resistance, eases one's passage through life. John's companion, Vertue, however, happened (fortuitously) to have read Aristotle and replied that his actual "doctrine of the Mean" differed from Sensible's, for Aristotle "specially says that there is no excess of goodness. You cannot go too far in the right direction."[20] Thus to be fully human means to be totally good! The final end, the real purpose, of life is to move as far as possible in the direction of goodness.

And that's what Jesus did, going all the way to the "good" from which He came. Christians thus affirm Christ's full humanity as well as His full deity. Jesus Christ is perfectly man as well as perfectly God. He was not an ethereal "god" walking on earth, magically materializing out of some cosmic mist, majestically moving to and fro, but the real God who became flesh. Nor did a man just like us named Jesus become the Logos, the Word of God. In fact, God's Logos became man like us. For He was born, as are we all, as a little baby. "That which was from the beginning, which we have heard, which we have seen with our eyes, which we have looked upon and touched with our hands, concerning the word of life" (1 John 1:1, RSV) is Christ Jesus.

In the Incarnation, God became man, assuming human nature in that miraculous condescension.

In the Incarnation, God became man, assuming human nature in that miraculous condescension. As medieval scholastics defined it: *assumptio carnis et animae*—Christ assumed our body and soul, lifting all that is ours as humans into himself. "Thereby," writes Karl Adam, "is sin taken from our nature. Man and sin are no longer identical."[21] We're no longer doomed to atrophy and die. Instead, we're free to become Christlike. "Hence Christ is our Redeemer, not in so far as he is God, nor in so far as he is Man, but because he is God-man, the new Adam."[22] As God's Son, sharing the very being of Yahweh himself, Christ Jesus salvaged human nature by refilling it with His divine presence—as if blood transfusion were given a dying patient, draining out the bad and replacing it with good. To fully redeem man, the eternal Word necessarily lifted unto himself, joined himself to, all that required redemption. Whatever needed sanctifying was assumed and transformed by the Incarnate Son. As Jesus Christ's brothers, joint-heirs with Him, we share the nature He assumed and made holy. Still, fully man, Jesus learned and obeyed and developed: he "increased in wisdom and in stature, and in favour with God and man" (Luke 2:52, KJV). Physically, psychologically, He was one with us. He felt joy and sorrow, comfort and pain. His family was much like ours— mom, dad, siblings—industriously working at daily tasks, enjoying the simple routines of everyday life.

Finally, His bond with us was fully evident in His death on the Cross. He bled and died as a man. He went through the "valley of the shadow of death." As Clement of Rome wrote, in the final years of the first century: "Because of the love He bore us, our Lord Jesus Christ, at the will of God, gave His blood for us—His flesh for our flesh, His life for our lives."[23]

20 ✏ Holy Spirit

"He Is Always Acting Through You"

> *This third Person is called . . . the Holy Ghost or
> the "spirit" of God. . . . In the Christian life you
> are not usually looking at Him: He is always act-*
> *ing through you. If you think of the Father as*
> *something "out there," in front of you, and of the
> Son as someone standing at your side, helping
> you to pray, trying to turn you into another son,
> then you have to think of the third Person as
> something inside you, or behind you.*[1]

A FEW YEARS AGO SOME BOYS, fulfilling a Sunday School class assignment, were reciting the Nicene Creed. The first boy said, "I believe in the Father Almighty, Maker of heaven and earth, and in all things visible and invisible." The second did equally well, saying, "I believe in one Lord, Jesus Christ . . ." and correctly finished his assignment, declaring His "kingdom shall have no end." Then, however, there was a long pause—somewhat like the silences that follow many of my questions in class! Finally one boy stepped forward and said to the teacher, "Sir, the boy who believes in the Holy Spirit is absent today."

What was true in that class has too often been true about the Church. We often refer to the Spirit, as part of the formulas we recite, but too often we have little clue as to who He really is. We teach much about the Father and the Son, but little about the Holy Spirit. This is, at first glance, as true of C. S. Lewis as of other Christian teachers. As he noted, the Spirit is "rather vaguer and more shadowy" than Father and Son. When you carefully peruse his works you encounter little specific discussion of the third Person of the Trinity.

> *We often refer to the Spirit,*
> *as part of the formulas we recite,*
> *but too often we have little clue*
> *as to who He really is.*

Yet, in her careful study of *Real Presence: The Holy Spirit in the Works of C. S. Lewis,* Leanne Payne insists the Holy Spirit is actually central to Lewis's thought. In her judgment, once one understands his terms, "Lewis has said much more about the Holy Spirit, and from a higher perspective . . . than many who write explicitly about Him today."[2] "For Lewis," she says, "to know God was to be invaded by His Spirit; as Christians we are both 'in Christ' and 'he in us.'"[3] This means that "the creature is linked to the Creator by the Spirit of the risen Christ. This fact, fully comprehended and experienced, is the 'whole of it' as Lewis would say. The kingdom has come among us and into us. To accept this truth is both to understand, and to know experientially, the presence of the Holy Spirit."[4]

Toward the end of *Out of the Silent Planet,* the first of Lewis's space stories, Elwin Ransom is brought before Oyarsa, the angelic ruler of Malacandra. The Malacandrians seemed to "see" him, but Ransom could only "sense" his presence. And it was very real! Trying to explain what he knew had transpired, something too marvelous for words, he said:

> The merest whisper of light—no, less than that, the smallest diminution of shadow—was travelling along the uneven surface of the ground-weed; or rather some difference in the look of the ground, too slight to be named in the language of the five senses, moved slowly towards him. Like a silence spreading over a room full of people, like an infinitesimal coolness on a sultry

day, like a passing memory of some long-forgotten
sound or scent, like all that is stillest and smallest and
most hard to seize in nature, Oyarsa passed between
his subjects and drew near and came to seat, not ten
yards away from Ransom in the centre of Meldilorn.
Ransom felt a tingling of his blood and a prickling on
his fingers as if lightning were near him; and his heart
and body seemed to him to be made of water.[5]

To try and grasp the essence of the Holy Spirit, like Ransom
trying to describe the very present Oyarsa, leads us to sing
songs and write poems. So to talk about the Spirit, and to find
some of Lewis's insights concerning the One who is, first of all,
holy, we will have to point to Him in conjunction with His mysterious workings in His world and our hearts, as well as envision Him as one of the three Persons in the holy communion of
persons we call Trinity.

In one of his letters, Lewis wondered at the ability of "higher"
powers to descend into "lower" powers, as the Oyarsa seemed
able to enter into the world of his subjects, the Malacandrians.
We know how unusually gifted musicians can explain the princi-
ples and beauty of music to less gifted persons. For years
Leonard Bernstein, orchestrating "concerts for young people,"
fascinated youthful audiences with his explanations of classical
music. Truly great philosophers, such as Aristotle, frequently explain their ideas much more clearly than the textbooks that pretend to simplify them. Thus, Lewis thought: "Adult minds (but
only the best of them) can descend into sympathy with children,
and men into sympathy with beasts," which means that "everything hangs together and the total reality, both Natural and Supernatural." So, "We catch sight of a new key principle—the
power of the Higher, just in so far as it is Higher, to come down,
the power of the greater to include the less."[6]

Centuries before Christ, the prophet Isaiah met God in the
Temple, somewhat as Ransom met the Oyarsa in Malacandra.
As Isaiah described it: "I saw the Lord seated on a throne, high
and exalted, and the train of his robe filled the temple" (6:1).
Six-winged angelic beings surrounded Him, "and they were call-
ing to one another: 'Holy, holy, holy is the LORD Almighty; the

whole earth is full of his glory'" (v. 3). This text opens one of our clearest windows into heavenly realms, unveiling diamond facets of God's essence. Centuries later, John, in Revelation, envisioned "four beasts [who] had each of them six wings about him; and they were full of eyes within: and they rest not day and night, saying, Holy, holy, holy, Lord God Almighty, which was, and is, and is to come" (4:8, KJV).

Now when a word is repeated in Scripture, as in daily discourse, it's usually to emphasize a truth. Jesus frequently said "truly, truly," to draw attention to His words. In the Old Testament, Gen. 14 records a battle where some men fell into tar pits. Translations say "asphalt" or "bitumen" or just "great pits." The Hebrew text, however, simply repeats one word: pit. They fell into a pit pit. When a word is repeated, it's for emphasis. And when a word was repeated three times, we're supposed to really wake up and pay attention. It's one thing to be in a pit pit. But it's utterly awful to be in a pitty pit pit! Thus when Isaiah, seeing God, said "holy, holy, holy," and John repeats it—declaring the *trishagion* (*tris* = three; *hagion* = holy)—we understand how important it is for us to revere a *holy God*. Indeed when we think "God," we must always think "holy," for He is, in essence, holy. And as a three-in-one Being He is, in each of three Persons, holy.

> *He is* pure, *and His most notable*
> *role in the workings of God is to*
> *sanctify with His presence . . .*
> *especially by cleansing sinful*
> *humans.*

This means, obviously, that the Holy Spirit, as God, is holy. Isaiah sensed this, for "at the sound of their voices [the seraphs singing 'holy, holy, holy'] the doorposts and thresholds shook and the temple was filled with smoke" (6:4). God is holy, and His Spirit is called the Holy Spirit. The Second Ecumenical

Council, held in Constantinople in 381, established the creed confessed by orthodox believers. It declares: "We believe in the Holy Spirit, the Lord and Giver of Life, who proceeds from the Father." Just as the Son is eternally begotten of the Father, so the Spirit eternally proceeds from the Father.

As we have seen, when discussing the Father and the Son in earlier chapters, holiness primarily refers to the divine *otherness,* the radical difference between God and His creatures. So the Holy Spirit is holy in that He is fully God, transcending in His being the world of creation. Second, He is also *pure,* and His most notable role in the workings of God is to sanctify with His presence all that is, especially by cleansing sinful humans.

Proceeding from the Father, the Spirit is God's will-in-action, the life-giving love shared and breathed out by God. In the King James Version, the Spirit is often called the Holy Ghost. The word *ghost* comes from an Anglo-Saxon word, *gast,* which came from an Old Norse word, *gustr.* We sometimes talk about a "gust" of wind—a sudden, powerful burst of power—which indicates the Spirit's presence. Lewis noted:

> **Confusion between Spirit and soul (or "ghost") has done much harm, for ghosts, unlike spirits, lack substance. Neither God nor even gods are "shadowy" in traditional imagination: even the human dead, when glorified in Christ, cease to be "ghosts" and become "saints." The difference of atmosphere which even now surrounds the words "I saw a ghost" and the words "I saw a saint"—all the pallor and insubstantiality of the one, all the gold and blue of the other—contains more wisdom than whole libraries of religion. If we must have a mental picture to symbolize Spirit, we should represent it as something heavier than matter.[7]**

In Lewis's judgment, this very real, thoroughly dense, energizing Holy Spirit "is perhaps the most important difference between Christianity and all other religions." The Christian God is not Aristotle's unmoved "Prime Mover" but One whose heart pulsates, pumping life-giving blood to all that lives. This will-in-action is the Spirit, just as truly a Person as the Father and the

Son. On a human level, we often talk about the "spirit" of a family, a college, a country. Such "communal" entities, what we call "spirit," take on a certain personality, to be sure. But they are not the kind of persons we are. They simply resemble us. "But that," Lewis says, "is just one of the differences between God and us. What grows out of the joint life of the Father and Son is a real Person, is in fact the Third of the three Persons who are God."[8]

God's Spirit, a "gust" from heaven, carries out God's loving will, brings about His designs. As a holy God, the Holy Spirit seeks to make holy His world. He is the Sanctifier, making holy all He indwells. So, Lewis, while admitting we cannot fully fathom a "three-personal Being," says, "The thing that matters is being actually drawn into that three-personal life." Thus, when a simple believer prays,

> **He is trying to get in touch with God. But if he is a Christian he knows that what is prompting him to pray is also God: God, so to speak, inside him. But he also knows that all his real knowledge of God comes through Christ, the Man who was God—that is Christ standing beside him, helping him to pray, praying for him. . . .**
>
> **The whole threefold life of the three-personal Being is actually going on in that ordinary little bedroom where an ordinary man is saying his prayers.**[9]

And it is, in prayer, that we truly sense the "bright shadow" of holiness that beckons us to enter into the joy of eternal life.

Notes

Preface

1. John Stackhouse Jr., "Movers and Shapers of Modern Evangelicalism," *Christianity Today,* September 16, 1996, 59.

2. Ibid., 59.

3. Charles Colson, "The Oxford Prophet," *Christianity Today,* June 15, 1998, 72.

4. Ibid.

Chapter 1

1. C. S. Lewis, *Surprised by Joy* (New York: Harcourt, Brace, 1955), 179.

2. Ibid., 181.

3. Ibid.

4. Ibid., 179.

5. C. S. Lewis, *The Great Divorce* (New York: Macmillan, 1946).

6. Ibid., 65.

7. Quoted in R. C. Sproul, *The Holiness of God* (Wheaton, Ill.: Tyndale House Publishers, 1985), 52.

8. C. S. Lewis, *Letters to an American Lady* (Grand Rapids: William. B. Eerdmans Publishing Co., 1967), 19.

9. Quoted in Sam Ervin, "Judicial Verbicide," in *Modern Age: The First Twenty-five Years,* ed. George A. Panichas (Indianapolis: Liberty Press, 1988), 456.

10. C. S. Lewis, *Studies in Words* (Cambridge: Cambridge University Press, 1960), 132.

11. Josef Pieper, "On Love," in *Faith, Hope, Love* (San Francisco: Ignatius Press, 1997), 147.

12. Lewis, *Studies in Words,* 173.

13. C. S. Lewis, "The Death of Words," in *Lewis on Stories* (New York: Harcourt Brace, 1982), 106-7.

14. Jonathan Edwards, *Religious Affections* (Portland: Multnomah Press, 1984), 79.

Chapter 2

1. C. S. Lewis, *Miracles* (New York: Macmillan Co., 1947), 89.

2. Gustaf Aulen, *The Faith of the Christian Church* (Philadelphia: Fortress Press, 1962), 103.

3. Thomas C. Oden, *The Living God* (San Francisco: Harper and Row, 1987), 100.

4. R. C. Sproul, *The Holiness of God,* 57.

5. Romano Guardini, *Learning the Virtues That Lead You to God* (Manchester, N.H.: Sophia Institute Press, 1998), vii.

6. Ibid., 9.

7. Gilbert Meilander, *The Theory and Practice of Virtue* (Notre Dame: University of Notre Dame Press, 1984), 68.

8. Quoted in Thomas L. Trevethan, *The Beauty of God's Holiness* (Downers Grove, Ill.: InterVarsity Press, 1995), 68.

9. Lewis, *Miracles,* 90.

10. Ibid.

11. Ibid.

12. Quoted in Trevethan, *The Beauty of God's Holiness,* 68.

13. C. S. Lewis, *The Problem of Pain* (London: Geoffrey Bles, 1942), 58.

14. Ibid.

15. C. S. Lewis, *Letters to Malcolm* (New York: Harcourt, Brace, and World, 1964), 86.

16. C. S. Lewis, "The Weight of Glory," in *The Weight of Glory and Other Addresses* (New York: Macmillan, 1949), 11.

17. Ibid.

18. Ibid., 13.

19. Ibid.

20. Ibid.

Chapter 3

1. C. S. Lewis, *Till We Have Faces* (New York: Harcourt, Brace, 1956), 279.

2. Plato, "Theaetetus," in *The Dialogues of Plato,* trans. Benjamin Jowett (Chicago: Encyclopaedia Britannica, 1952), 519.

3. Aristotle, "Metaphysics," in *The Works of Aristotle,* trans. W. D. Ross (Chicago: Encyclopaedia Britannica, 1952), 1:500-501.

4. C. S. Lewis, *The Pilgrim's Regress* (New York: Sheed, 1935), 129.

5. C. S. Lewis, "Is Theism Important?" in *God in the Dock* (Grand Rapids: William B. Eerdmans Publishing Co., 1970), 174.

6. Ibid.

7. Lewis, *Till We Have Faces,* 308.

8. Gregory of Nyssa, *The Life of Moses* (New York: Paulist Press, 1987), 60.

9. Martin Buber, *Ten Rungs: Hasidic Sayings* (New York: Schocken Books, 1947), 15.

10. Lewis, *Letters to Malcolm,* 21.

11. Buber, *Ten Rungs,* 15.

12. Lewis, *Letters to Malcolm,* 75.

13. Ibid., 79-80.

14. Ibid., 81.

15. Ibid., 82.

16. Ibid.

Chapter 4

1. Lewis, *Pilgrim's Regress,* 13.

2. C. S. Lewis, *The Screwtape Letters* (London: Geoffrey Bles, 1942), 64.

3. Peter Kreeft, *C. S. Lewis for the Third Millennium* (San Francisco: Ignatius Press, 1994), 151.

4. Thomas Aquinas, *Light of Faith: The Compendium of Theology* (Manchester, N.H.: Sophia Institute Press, 1993), 109.

5. Ibid., 113.

6. C. S. Lewis, *Prince Caspian* (New York: Macmillan, 1951), 212.

7. Lewis, *Weight of Glory,* 19.

8. Ibid., 18.

9. Aquinas, *Light of Faith,* 72.

10. Josef Pieper, *The Silence of St. Thomas* (Chicago: Henry Regnery, 1957), 96.

11. C. S. Lewis, *Abolition of Man* (New York: Macmillan, 1947), 88.

12. Plato, "Theaetetus," in *The Dialogues of Plato,* Encyclopaedia Britannica, 176b.

13. Ashley Brilliant, *All I Want Is a Warm Bed and a Kind Word* (Santa Barbara, Calif.: Woodbridge Press, 1985), 81.

14. Lewis, "Dogma and the Universe," in *God in the Dock,* 41-42.

15. Lewis, "Man or Rabbit," in *God in the Dock,* 108.

16. C. S. Lewis, *Poems* (New York: Harcourt, Brace, Jovanovich, 1977), 81.

17. Lewis, *Screwtape Letters,* 8.

18. Kevin Graham Ford and James Denney, *Jesus for a New Generation: Putting the Gospel in the Language of Xers* (Downers Grove, Ill.: InterVarsity Press, 1995), 56.

19. Ibid., 55.

20. Ibid., 116.

21. Ibid., 130.

22. Peter Sacks, *Generation X Goes to College: An Eye-Opening Account of Teaching in Postmodern America* (Chicago: Open Court, 1996), 108.

23. Ibid., 110.

24. Ibid., 118.

25. Ibid., 143.

26. Ibid., 148.

27. Lewis, *Miracles,* 23.

28. Ibid., 19-20.

29. C. S. Lewis, *Mere Christianity* (New York: Macmillan Co., 1966), 52-53.

30. Lewis, *Screwtape Letters,* 46.

Chapter 5

1. Lewis, *Screwtape Letters,* 25.

2. C. S. Lewis, "On Stories" in *Of Other Worlds: Essays and Stories* (New York: Harcourt, Brace, Jovanovich, 1966), 15.

3. Thomas Howard, *The Achievement of C. S. Lewis* (Wheaton, Ill.: Harold Shaw Publishers, 1980), 107-8.

4. C. S. Lewis, *Perelandra* (New York: Macmillan Co., 1944), 142.

5. Aquinas, *Light of Faith,* 72.

6. Lewis, *Screwtape Letters,* 19.

7. Quoted in David Dooley, *G. K. Chesterton: Collected Works* (San Francisco: Ignatius Press, 1986), 1:14.

8. Quoted in Robert A. Sungenesis, *Not by Faith Alone* (Santa Barbara, Calif.: Queenship Publishing Co., 1997), 653.

9. Ibid., 454.

10. John Calvin, *Institutes of the Christian Religion* (Grand Rapids: William B. Eerdmans Publishing Co., 1947), 3:21.

11. Lewis, "The Trouble with 'X,'" in *God in the Dock,* 152-53.

12. Andre Gide, *The Immoralist* (New York: A. A. Knopf, 1930), 1:1.

13. Lewis, *Problem of Pain,* 69.

14. Albert Camus, *Resistance, Rebellion, and Death* (New York: Knopf, 1961).

15. C. S. Lewis, *Mere Christianity,* 52.

16. C. S. Lewis, *Out of the Silent Planet* (New York: Macmillan, 1943), 102.

17. Lewis, *Screwtape Letters,* 24.

18. Lewis, *Mere Christianity,* 52.

19. C. S. Lewis, *Four Loves* (New York: Harcourt, Brace, Jovanovich, 1960), 16-17.

20. Ibid.

21. Quoted in Roger L. Green and Walter Hooper, *C. S. Lewis: A Biography* (N.Y.: Harcourt Brace and Company, 1994), 202.

22. Ibid., 202.

23. Lewis, *Mere Christianity,* 21.

24. Ibid., 124.

25. Irenaeus, *Against Heresies* (Oxford: Clarendon Press, 1874), 37.

Chapter 6

1. Lewis, *Letters to Malcolm,* 69.

2. Quoted in Cornelius Plantinga Jr., *Not the Way It's Supposed to Be: A Breviary of Sin* (Grand Rapids: William B. Eerdmans Publishing Co., 1994), 7.

3. Phyllis McGinley, Introduction to C. S. Lewis, *The Screwtape Letters* (New York: Time Incorporated, 1963), xvii.

4. Ibid.

5. C. S. Lewis, "The Seeing Eye," in *Christian Reflections* (Grand Rapids: William B. Eerdmans Publishing Co., 1967), 168-69.

6. Quoted in C. S. Lewis, *A Preface to Paradise Lost* (New York: Oxford University Press, 1961), 66.

7. Quoted in ibid.

8. Ibid.

9. Quoted in Ibid.

10. Ibid., 67.

11. Lewis, *Mere Christianity,* 89-90.

12. Lewis, *Letters to Malcolm,* 69.

13. Lewis, *Mere Christianity,* 49.

14. Iris Murdoch, "On 'God' and 'Good,'" in *Revisions: Changing Perspectives in Moral Philosophy,* ed. Stanley Hauerwas and Alasdair MacIntyre (Notre Dame: University of Notre Dame Press, 1983), 78.

15. Lewis, *Preface to Paradise Lost,* 97.

16. C. S. Lewis, *The Last Battle* (New York: Collier Books, 1986), 33.

17. Ibid., 102.

Chapter 7

1. C. S. Lewis, *The Magician's Nephew* (New York: Macmillan Co., 1955), 72.

2. Ibid., 112.

3. Lewis, "Membership," in *Weight of Glory,* 118.

4. Lewis, *Screwtape Letters,* vii.

5. Ibid., xxvi.

6. Lewis, *Magician's Nephew,* 18.

7. Ibid.

8. Ibid.

9. C. S. Lewis, *The Lion, the Witch, and the Wardrobe* (New York: Macmillan, 1950), 62.

10. Ibid.

11. Ibid., 38.

12. Lewis, *Screwtape Letters,* ix.

13. Francisco de Osuna, *The Third Spiritual Alphabet,* trans. Mary E. Giles (New York: Paulist Press, 1981), 202.

14. Ibid., 203.

15. Peter Kreeft, *Making Choices: Practical Wisdom for Everyday Moral Decisions* (Ann Arbor, Mich.: Servant Books, 1990), 176.

16. C. S. Lewis, *The Silver Chair* (New York: Macmillan Co., 1953), 153.

17. Ibid., 155.

18. Ibid., 156.

19. Lewis, *Out of the Silent Planet,* 110.

20. Ibid., 111-12.

21. Lewis, *Mere Christianity,* 51.

Chapter 8

1. George MacDonald quoted in Lewis, *Surprised by Joy,* 212.

2. Lewis, *Problem of Pain,* 135.

3. John Wesley, *Works,* vol. XI (1872; reprint, Kansas City: Beacon Hill Press of Kansas City, 1979), 395.

4. Lewis, *Problem of Pain,* 69.

5. C. S. Lewis, "Religion: Reality or Substitute?" in *Christian Reflections,* 39.

6. Lewis, *Prince Caspian,* 35.

7. Lewis, *Problem of Pain,* 70.

8. Lewis, *Preface to Paradise Lost,* 70.

9. Ibid., 70-71.

10. Lewis, *Out of the Silent Planet,* 122.

11. Lewis, *Screwtape Letters,* 28.

12. Lewis, *Pilgrim's Regress,* 177.

13. Lewis, *Screwtape Letters,* 68.

14. Quoted in Irving Kristol, *Neo-Conservatism* (New York: The Free Press, 1995), 193.

15. Lewis, *Screwtape Letters,* 69.

16. Lewis, *Perelandra,* 208.

17. Ibid.

18. Ibid.

19. Lewis, *Problem of Pain,* 127.

Chapter 9

1. C. S. Lewis, *That Hideous Strength* (New York: Macmillan Co., 1946), 288-89.

2. Meredith Veldman, *Fantasy, the Bomb, and the Greening of Britain: Romantic Protest, 1945-1980* (Cambridge: Cambridge University Press, 1994).

3. Ibid., 2.

4. Ibid., 37.

5. Lewis, *That Hideous Strength,* 42.

6. Ibid.

7. Ibid.

8. Ibid., 172-73.

9. Hilary Putnam, *Reason, Truth, and History* (Cambridge: Cambridge University Press, 1981), 40.

10. William P. Alston, *A Realist Conception of Truth* (Ithaca, N.Y.: Cornell University Press, 1996).

11. Ibid., 264.

12. Ibid.

13. John Donne, "An Anatomie of the World," in *John Donne: Selected Poetry,* ed. Marius Beverley (New York: New American Library, c. 1966), 211.

14. William Butler Yeats, "The Second Coming," in *The Poems of W. B. Yeats: A New Edition,* ed. Richard J. Finneran (New York: Macmillan Publishing Co., 1924), 187.

15. Lewis, *Abolition of Man,* 88.

16. Ibid., 26.

17. Ibid., 28.

18. Lewis, *Out of the Silent Planet,* 153.

19. Lewis, *Pilgrim's Regress,* 187.

20. David Ehrenfeld, *The Arrogance of Humanism* (New York: Oxford University Press, 1978), 16-17.

Chapter 10

1. Lewis, *Mere Christianity,* 77.

2. C. S. Lewis, "Democratic Education," in *Present Concerns* (San Diego: Harcourt, Brace, Jovanovich, 1986), 34.

3. Lewis, *Screwtape Letters,* 164-68.

4. Ibid., 64.

5. Lewis, *Surprised by Joy,* 179.

6. Lewis, *Screwtape Letters,* 123.

7. Lewis, *Mere Christianity,* 175.

Chapter 11

1. Lewis, *Mere Christianity,* 169.

2. Lewis, *Letters to Malcolm,* 5.

3. Quoted in Gilbert Meilander, *The Taste for the Other* (Grand Rapids: William B. Eerdmans Publishing Co., 1978), 122.

4. *Catechism of the Catholic Church* (Boston: St. Paul Books and Media, 1994), 170-71.

5. Meilander, *The Taste for the Other,* 122.

6. Lewis, *Mere Christianity,* 171.

7. Lewis, "Man or Rabbit," in *God in the Dock,* 112.

8. Ibid.

9. Lewis, *Mere Christianity,* 171.

10. Ibid., 139-40.

11. Lewis, *The Voyage of the Dawn Treader* (New York: Macmillan Co., 1952), 89.

12. Ibid., 89-91.

13. Ibid., 93.

Chapter 12

1. Lewis, *Mere Christianity,* 62.
2. Ibid., 155.
3. Lewis, *Miracles,* 178.
4. Leo Tolstoy, *"A Confession" and "What I Believe,"* trans. Aylmer Maude (London: Oxford University Press, 1940), 15.
5. Ibid., 31.
6. Lewis, *Mere Christianity,* 137-38.
7. Ibid., 183.
8. Lewis, "Membership," in *Weight of Glory,* 119.
9. Lewis, *Mere Christianity,* 155.
10. Lewis, "Membership," in *Weight of Glory,* 112.
11. Lewis, *Mere Christianity,* 64-65.
12. Ibid., 153.
13. Ibid., 85.
14. Ibid., 154.
15. Ibid., 182.
16. Lewis, *That Hideous Strength,* 177.
17. Ibid., 360.

Chapter 13

1. Lewis, *Screwtape Letters,* 40.
2. Lewis, "The Decline of Religion," in *God in the Dock,* 221.
3. Lewis, *Till We Have Faces,* 282-83.
4. Ibid., 254.
5. Ibid., 166.
6. Ibid., 279.
7. Ibid., 280.
8. Ibid., 291.
9. Ibid., 291-92.
10. Ibid., 294.
11. Ibid.
12. Ibid., 307
13. Ibid., 308.
14. Lewis, *Perelandra,* 142.
15. Ibid.
16. Ibid.
17. Ibid., 146.
18. Lewis, "The Decline of Religion," in *God in the Dock,* 221.
19. Lewis, *Mere Christianity,* 52.

Chapter 14

1. Lewis, *Mere Christianity,* 167.

2. Lewis, *Reflections on the Psalms* (New York: Harcourt, Brace, 1958), 31-32.

3. Quoted in Eugene Peterson, *A Long Obedience in the Same Direction* (Downer's Grove, Ill.: InterVarsity Press, 1980), 8.

4. Lewis, *Mere Christianity,* 171.

5. Ibid., 172.

6. C. S. Lewis, *The Horse and His Boy* (New York: Macmillan Co., 1954), 193.

7. Ibid.

8. Lewis, *Mere Christianity,* 190.

9. Ibid.

10. Lewis, *That Hideous Strength,* 115.

11. Ibid.

12. Ibid., 73.

13. Ibid., 147.

14. Daphne Hampson, *Theology and Feminism* (Oxford: Blackwell, 1990), 123.

15. Lewis, *That Hideous Strength,* 142.

16. Ibid., 143.

17. Ibid., 151.

18. Lewis, *Mere Christianity,* 114.

Chapter 15

1. Warren H. Lewis, ed., *Letters of C. S. Lewis* (New York: Harcourt, Brace, and World, 1966), 225.

2. Lewis, *Great Divorce,* 69.

3. Ibid., 72-73.

4. Ibid., 69.

5. Lewis, *Problem of Pain,* 118-19.

6. Lewis, *Perelandra,* 208.

7. Lewis, *Silver Chair,* 146.

8. Lewis, *Problem of Pain,* 90.

9. Ibid.

10. Ibid., 90-91.

11. Lewis, *That Hideous Strength,* 149.

12. Lewis, "Membership," in *Weight of Glory,* 113.

Chapter 16

1. Lewis, *Mere Christianity,* 161.

2. Ibid., 188.

3. Lewis, *Weight of Glory,* 27-28.

4. Lewis, *Mere Christianity,* 187.

5. Lewis, "Membership," in *Weight of Glory,* 116.

6. C. S. Lewis, "Undeceptions," quoted in Christopher Derrick, *C. S.*

Lewis and the Church of the Rome (San Francisco: Ignatius Press, 1981), 143.

7. Lewis, "To a Lady," in *Letters,* 224.
8. Lewis, *That Hideous Strength,* 78.
9. Ibid.
10. Ibid., 79.
11. Lewis, *Mere Christianity,* 12.
12. Ibid., 186.
13. Ibid., 169-70.

Chapter 17

1. Lewis, "As the Ruin Falls," in *Poems,* 109-10.
2. Lewis, *Mere Christianity,* 181.
3. Quoted in *The New York Times,* March 7, 1962.
4. R. L. Green and Walter Hooper, *C. S. Lewis: A Biography,* 106.
5. Lewis, *Mere Christianity,* 118-19.
6. Augustine, "The City of God," in *Nicene and Post-Nicene Fathers,* ed. Phillip Schaff (Peabody, Mass.: Hendrickson Publishers, Inc., 1995), 1:6.
7. Lewis, *Problem of Pain,* 92.
8. Ibid., 92-93.
9. Ibid., 95.
10. Ibid., 95-96.
11. Lewis, *Letters of C. S. Lewis,* 257.
12. Lewis, *A Grief Observed* (New York: Seabury, 1964), 50.
13. Ibid., 51.
14. Ibid., 49-50.
15. Lewis, *Letters of C. S. Lewis,* 237-38.
16. Ibid.
17. Lewis, *Miracles,* 130.
18. Ibid.
19. Lewis, *Out of the Silent Planet,* 140.
20. Lewis, *Miracles,* 130.
21. Ibid.

Chapter 18

1. Lewis, *Miracles,* 84-85.
2. David Blankenhorn, *Fatherless America* (New York: BasicBooks, 1995), 1.
3. Ibid., 5.
4. "Hallowed Be Thy Name," *Newsweek* (June 17, 1996), 75.
5. C. S. Lewis, *Miracles,* 82.
6. Ibid., 82-83.
7. Ibid., 93.
8. Lewis, *Mere Christianity,* 135.

9. Quoted in Peter Toon, *Yesterday, Today, and Forever: Jesus Christ and the Holy Trinity in the Teaching of the Seven Ecumenical Councils* (Swedesboro, N.J.: Preservation Press, 1996), 210.

10. Lewis, *Mere Christianity,* 144.

11. Donald Bloesch, *The Battle for the Trinity* (Ann Arbor, Mich.: Servant Publications, 1985), 35.

12. Ibid.

13. Augustine, "Homilies on the Gospel of St. John," in *Nicene and Post-Nicene Fathers,* 7:124.

14. Ibid.

15. Lewis, *God in the Dock,* 237.

16. Bloesch, *Battle for the Trinity,* 11.

17. Lewis, *God in the Dock,* 237.

18. Ibid., 238.

19. Manfred Hauke, *God or Goddess?* (San Francisco: Ignatius Press, 1995), 127.

20. Lewis, *That Hideous Strength,* 13.

21. Lewis, *Perelandra,* 200.

22. Ibid.

23. Lewis, *Miracles,* 91.

24. Lewis, *The Discarded Image* (Cambridge, England: Cambridge University Press, 1964), 37.

25. Bloesch, *Battle for the Trinity,* 54.

26. Lewis, *Miracles,* 94.

27. "Hymns for the Politically Correct," *Christianity Today* (July 15, 1996), 49.

Chapter 19

1. Lewis, *The Lion, the Witch, and the Wardrobe,* 75-76.

2. Lewis, *Mere Christianity,* 46.

3. Michael Davies, ed., *Newman Against the Liberals* (Harrison, N.Y.: Roman Catholic Books, 1978), 13.

4. Lewis, *Letters to Malcolm,* 118-19.

5. H. Richard Niebuhr, *The Kingdom of God in America* (New York: Harper and Bros., 1959), 193.

6. Lewis, *The Lion, the Witch, and the Wardrobe,* 123.

7. Augustine, "Homilies on the Gospel of St. John," in *Nicene and Post-Nicene Fathers,* 7:58.

8. Aquinas, *Light of Faith,* 312.

9. Lewis, *The Lion, the Witch, and the Wardrobe,* 76.

10. Lewis, *Prince Caspian,* 199-200.

11. Ibid., 209.

12. Ibid., 210.

13. Lewis, *Four Loves,* 81.

14. Lewis, *Pilgrim's Regress,* 79.

15. Ibid., 14.

16. C. S. Lewis, *Letters: C. S. Lewis/Don Giovanni Calabria* (Ann Arbor, Mich.: Servant Books, 1988), 57.

17. Eugene Peterson, *Take and Read* (Grand Rapids: William B. Eerdmans Publishing Company, 1996), 91.

18. Augustine, *Predestination of Saints* (Washington, D.C.: Catholic University of America Press, 1992), 513.

19. Lewis, *Pilgrim's Regress,* 85.

20. Ibid., 86.

21. Karl Adam, *The Son of God* (Garden City: Image Books, 1960), 16.

22. Ibid.

23. Clement of Rome, *First Epistle of Clement* in *Anti-Nicene Fathers* (Grand Rapids: William B. Eerdmans, 1981), 1.49.18.

Chapter 20

1. Lewis, *Mere Christianity,* 152.

2. Leanne Payne, *Real Presence: The Holy Spirit in the Works of C. S. Lewis* (Westchester, Ill.: Cornerstone Books, 1979), 15.

3. Ibid., 14.

4. Ibid., 14-15.

5. Lewis, *Out of the Silent Planet,* 119.

6. Quoted in Payne, *Real Presence,* 48-49.

7. Lewis, *Miracles,* 92.

8. Lewis, *Mere Christianity,* 152.

9. Ibid., 142-43.